WHAT IS LINGUISTICS?

WHAT IS LINGUISTICS?

Third Edition

DAVID CRYSTAL

Reader in Linguistic Science, University of Reading

EDWARD ARNOLD

© DAVID CRYSTAL 1974
First published 1968 by
Edward Arnold (Publishers) Ltd.
25 Hill Street, London W1X 8LL
Second edition, 1969
Reprinted with amendments 1971
Third edition, 1974

Boards edition ISBN: 0 7131 5740 2
Paper edition ISBN: 0 7131 5741 0

Printed in Great Britain by
The Camelot Press Ltd., London and Southampton

Contents

Preface

This book tries to introduce a new and rapidly developing subject to people who have perhaps heard only the name Linguistics before, who do not know what it means, and who are not even sure that they want to know. I have tried to talk around the subject in a very general way, so that people can find out what it is about reasonably quickly and cheaply, and thus make up their own minds whether they want to study it in more detail. My aim is not to write a comprehensive introduction to Linguistics. It does not take a large, systematic survey of the subject to answer the simple question 'What is Linguistics?'. Professional linguists frequently have to give thumb-nail sketches of their subject to people they meet, and little more than this is required. I have assumed complete ignorance of the subject on the part of my reader, and tried to take nothing for granted. Those who have some knowledge of Linguistics already must bear with this principle, for this book was not written for them.

I have found the question 'What is Linguistics?' coming at me from five distinct sources, and I have thus five separate audiences in mind. First, it is asked by the sixth-former, who is about to apply for a university place, who sees Linguistics in a prospectus, and begins to wonder whether this might not be for him. Second, it is asked by the first-year undergraduate, who has arrived at a university to read, say, English, or Modern Languages, and who finds that he can take Linguistics as part of his course, if he wishes. Third, it is asked by the foreign student of English, because it is in the large field of teaching English as a foreign language that the word Linguistics is most frequently heard. Fourth, it is asked by the 'interested general reader', who can always be safely invoked in a Preface, but who in this case is a very important audience, in view of the centrality of language in relation to very many areas of human behaviour. And fifth, it is asked by teachers who have come across the subject in the course of their work for the first time.

The book is in three sections. Chapter 1 looks at some of the current misconceptions about Linguistics and language, and tries to relate the modern study of language to some of the older approaches. Chapter 2 discusses the implications of the phrase 'a science of language', and examines some aspects of the complexity of language's form and function. Chapter 3 then looks at the uses Linguistics has in society, and the kind of job one can expect to do with a qualification in the subject. The book explains my own view as to what Linguistics is about, but I have tried to restrict my attention to matters which would generally be considered to be unoriginal and orthodox. Other authors would certainly have placed the emphasis in different places, however, and so, to provide further perspective in the subject, as well as to assist those who would like to carry on with their study of Linguistics, I have given information about further reading in Appendix A. In Appendix B, I have added some details of courses leading to a degree involving Linguistics at several British universities.

Preface to the second edition

For this edition, a number of minor changes have been made in the body of the text in order to clarify points of detail. Appendix B has doubled in length, reflecting the developing recognition of Linguistics as an academic discipline by many universities; also, some of the courses given in the First Edition have been altered by departments, experience suggesting improvements in the range and depth of the degrees, and these alterations have been incorporated.   D.C.

May, 1969

Preface to the third edition

The two Appendices have undergone further changes for this edition. Some recently published items have been added to the reading list, and the list of University courses has been considerably revised and expanded. Once again, the number of courses available has nearly doubled—but it is interesting to note that the area of expansion has been almost entirely in the provision of Combined Subject degrees. There seems to be a definite tendency now for University work in Linguistics to concentrate on seeing the subject as foundation and perspective for coursework in other fields, especially modern languages, and some Departments have in fact taken pains to draw attention to this in their prospectuses. The same emphasis applies to the introduction of the subject into colleges of education, where since 1969 the progress of the subject has been quite considerable, as part of degrees and certificates in Education. The comment on p. 1 about 'other institutions' should therefore be interpreted accordingly. And lastly, I ought to draw attention to the emphasis placed upon Linguistics in the Report of the Committee which investigated speech therapy in this country (*Speech Therapy Services*, H.M.S.O., 1972), and which saw language as the 'central core' of the therapist's discipline, and linguistics as one of its foundation subjects. It seems clear that, if *What is Linguistics?* were being written in 1973, I would need to spend a great deal more space on the implications of Chapter 3. Hopefully, the additional reading in Appendix A will make good this gap.

October, 1973

CHAPTER ONE

What Linguistics is Not

'Linguistics' is a word which seems particularly prone to mis-interpretation. To begin with, when people hear the name for the first time, they usually do not ask 'What *is* Linguistics?', but 'What *are* Linguistics?'—as if the word referred to a collection of 'linguisticky' objects conveniently gathered together for examination, like pictures at an exhibition. It is not really surprising, though, that people should react in this way, and treat the noun as if it were a 'thing' word like 'car', rather than a 'mass' one like 'mathematics'. The subject has not been in existence long enough to be generally recognized as the name of an intellectual discipline. It has been studied in an academic context only since the turn of the century, and it has really developed in British universities only since about 1960. It has been going longer in the United States, but even there study is restricted almost entirely to the postgraduate level. In Britain, the first under-graduate degree courses (always a significant stage in the development of a subject) were begun as recently as 1964, at York leading to a B.A. in Language, and in 1965 at Reading leading to a B.A. in Linguistics; and while the subject is rapidly gaining ground in the universities (see Appendix B), it has not yet made much progress in other institutes of higher education or in the schools.

The relative newness of the subject creates a problem, however. For if someone does come across the word (in a university prospectus, for example), and wants to know more about it, where can he go? He might try the relevant volume of the *Oxford English Dictionary*, but this will not get him very far: this soberly informs him that *linguistics* is 'the science of languages; philology', that a *linguistician* is 'one who is versed in linguistics', and that a *linguist* is 'one who is skilled in the use of languages; one who is master of other tongues beside his own'. The trouble with these definitions is that they are almost completely wrong, as far as the modern academic study called Linguistics (or General Linguistics, or Linguistic Science) is concerned. We shall be discussing some of the reasons for this shortly. The sense of *Linguist* as 'a student of language', which is nearer the mark, is in fact classed as 'obsolete' by the *O.E.D.*! And if the enquirer looks at a more recently revised dictionary, such as the *Third Webster International Dictionary*, he will certainly find more up-to-date information, but the glosses are sufficiently technical for him still to require substantial clarification. So where else can he turn? If he is lucky, there may be a careers master at school, or a helpful librarian in the locality, who may have read a little in the subject and can inform. But what if there is not? Or if the enquirer *is* a careers master or a helpful librarian, and does not know?

There are a number of difficulties in the way of anyone trying to discover what Linguistics is about, and these have to be admitted and faced. For one thing the relatively recent growth of the subject means that very few introductory textbooks have been produced; and of those that are available, many suffer from what, for the *complete* beginner, are faults. They tend to be too comprehensive in scope, rather advanced in level, and frequently rather unreadable. To take the point about comprehensiveness first, it is surely the case that a relatively complete survey of Linguistics is far too ambitious for one's first reading in the subject; after all, this assumes an acquired interest, and a desire on the part of an individual to go into it in some depth. When one sees that R. A. Hall's *Introductory Linguistics* is some 500 pages long, for example, then it should be clear that this is a very serious sense of 'introductory', which assumes either considerable interest, or at least compulsory attendance at a course of study, before one plunges in. But what about those people—in my view the majority—who are not yet sure that Linguistics is even potentially interesting or useful? What we lack are brief, introductory accounts of the subject for people who want to know what it is about without having to commit themselves to a course of serious study—and I am not able to recommend at the time of writing any book on Linguistics which could safely be called bedtime reading.

As regards level, many of the introductory books currently available are hardly introductory in the sense that they could be read without a supervisor. Linguists tend to forget the great gap which exists between their study of language and the views of the man in the street. They often take too much for granted, introduce technical terms with too little explanation, or focus their attention on relatively specialist or restricted areas of study. The word 'introductory' or 'introduction' in a title covers a multitude of sins, and does not really guarantee anything. Nor, incidentally, do books simply entitled 'language'. If one dips into the literature without advice, one can get into very deep water very quickly: witness the confusion of a sixth-former who came for a university interview in Linguistics having begun to read a book with the deceptive title *Fundamentals of Language*—a book which is in fact recommended reading for advanced postgraduate students. Also, the books which do appear in public libraries tend to be the wrong ones, popular and often misleading accounts of the less important, and usually less technical sides of Linguistics, as far as its university study goes. Books like *The Loom of Language* by F. Bodmer and L. Hogben or *The Story of Language* by Mario Pei, though interesting in many ways, embody a number of misconceptions, and do not really give a clear picture of what is expected of someone about to take up the study of Linguistics seriously. What we need are reliable popularizations to enable one to get the feel of the subject relatively quickly, without having to assimilate too much new information at once—yet providing enough to allow him to make up his mind that Linguistics is or is not a good thing to (*a*) begin studying, (*b*) apply to a university to read, or (*c*) bring into a modern language course, and so on. And until such are written, the problem for the beginner will remain.

A more worrying point, relating in a way to the *O.E.D.* definitions, is that many people see the word 'Linguistics', and assume that they know what it means, while in fact they do not. The general reaction, as far as I can see, is to equate Linguistics with Philology, the study of the history of language, and to discuss it only in these terms when giving someone advice. To illustrate this point, we may take the case of the sixth-formers who applied to read Linguistics at Reading University in 1967, the first year the subject was offered by the University in the U.C.C.A. prospectus. *All* applicants, when asked what they thought the study of Linguistics was, began to talk about such things as the way words and meanings change over the years, or how languages originated in the history of mankind. Now they must have got this view from somewhere, and the consistency of their replies argues a quite general misconception as to what language study is centrally about. Their answer is of course only a very small part of the truth. And if they believe this answer—and why shouldn't they?—then whichever attitude they adopt, the result is potentially unfortunate: those who do not like historical studies may be put off Linguistics for good, and never know what they are missing; and those who do, when they begin the non-historical work which is so much a part of modern Linguistics, may get a rude shock.

There is also a danger, unhappily, that prospective students may ask advice from someone who knows about Linguistics, but who has at some time or another been offended by the subject. These people are quite numerous, in fact. The history of Linguistics, as of many new sciences, has been filled with clashes between disciplines, while the subject extended its field of study. A lot of this was due to exaggerated claims on behalf of Linguistics—claiming, for example, that one could not study the

Classics without linguistic training, or that literary criticism was all wrong unless a thorough linguistic study of a text had first been made. But much was due to uncritical conservatism in people who worked in more well-established fields of study, and who did not like the critical examination which Linguistics was making of many cherished ideas. Nowadays, people pride themselves on being more enlightened and ecumenical in their views on the relationship of Linguistics to other subjects, but feelings can still be aroused. Moral: if one finds a person who reacts violently when asked what Linguistics is about, one should nod politely and ask someone else.

There are, then, numerous misconceptions about the nature of Linguistics, and it may be as well to get these out of the way once and for all. Let us say, therefore, forcibly, that Linguistics is *not* to be identified with four main fields: (*a*) comparative philology, or philology, or the study of the history of language, or whatever one likes to call it; (*b*) the learning of many languages, or polyglottism; (*c*) literary criticism, or other fields involving a scale of values, such as speech-training; and (*d*) the traditional study of grammar as carried on over the past hundred years in most of our schools. I shall amplify each of these points before going on to be a bit more constructive as to what Linguistics is.

Firstly, Linguistics is not to be viewed as a historical (or *diachronic*) study. In a historical study of language, we see how different languages have developed from older languages, such as English from Old English (or Anglo-Saxon, as it is often called), or French from Latin, and how these older languages in turn have developed from still earlier languages, which perhaps no longer exist—for example, Latin, Greek and Sanskrit from the language we call Indo-European. We do not, incidentally, deal with such dramatic problems as the origin of language, or the world's first language, in view of the fact that there is hardly any evidence we can point to in order to solve such questions scientifically. 'Comparative philology' is a branch of linguistic study which has been practised in an amateurish kind of way for many hundreds of years, though not systematically until the end of the eighteenth century. It is, however, only one aspect of Linguistics as a whole—and really quite a small, though complex one. (Historical studies account for but one paper out of nine in the present Final Examination at Reading University, for example.) We shall (see p. 27) define Linguistics as 'the science of language', and clearly there is a lot more to language, or to any other phenomenon, than its history. Linguistics is in fact primarily concerned with the *non*-historical (i.e. *synchronic*) study of language, the study of a state of a language at a given time, seen regardless of its previous or future history: to look, for instance, at English as it is used now, in the 1960s, or as it was in Shakespeare's time, and not at the way in which Shakespeare's English *became* modern English, or the way in which English current today is even now in the process of changing into the English of the twenty-first century. Most of the important questions which the linguist asks about language are not historical questions at all. What are the jobs that language does in society? How does it do them? How do we analyse any language which we come across? Do all languages have the same parts of speech? What is the relationship between language and thought? Or language and literature? To answer such questions, and many more besides, we are forced to look at language in a non-historical way, to see it as an object of study which has to be examined empirically, in its own terms, like the subject-matter of physics or chemistry.

Secondly, Linguistics is not to be interpreted as language learning or teaching. A 'linguist', in our sense, is not a man who has a skill in using many languages, though this sense is of course a current one for the word. One of the most frequent conversations that I have is based on this ambiguity. It runs as follows.
Interlocutor: You're at the University, are you? (*Friendly smile*) And what do you do there?
Self: I teach Linguistics.

Interlocutor (Face drops): Oh. And how many languages do you speak?

This is a difficult conversation to continue. Few professional linguists are actually *fluent* in more than one language. In trying to answer, I attempt to point out that it is not a question of 'speaking' a language which makes a man a linguist, in our sense, but of being able to 'speak *about*' a language, of knowing about the principles on which languages can be said to work, and about the kinds of difference which exist between one language and another. Moreover, the number of languages which a linguist will 'know about' in some degree of detail will vary from one year to the next, and depend largely on the kind of students he has at any one time, and the kind of interests they have. For example, if I have a student who for some reason wants to do some work on, say, an African language like Twi, then, unless I can refer him to a colleague who is a Twi specialist, I have simply got to begin studying this language myself, so that I can help him find his way about in it. By examples such as this, I would point out to my interlocutor that what Linguistics really gives one is an ability to approach the study of language confidently and methodically; it inculcates an analytic state of mind towards all kinds of things which take place in language; and while it certainly does improve one's ability to learn new languages, this is a by-product of the training one receives, and quite incidental. But such arguments interlocutors usually have no time or desire to hear. More often than not in a conversation of this kind these days, I do not try to explain my sense of 'linguist' along these lines, but in answer to the question 'How many languages do you speak?' simply answer, tongue in cheek, 'twenty-eight'!

Thirdly, Linguistics is not concerned with evaluating language in use. The linguist does not try to do the job of the literary critic, for example, who is indeed also concerned with the uses of language, but at an entirely different level. The linguist is often interested in studying the kind of language used in literary texts, it is true, but this does not turn him into a critic. The difference is simply that when the linguist looks at language in use, he is simply concerned with describing the *facts* of the utterances, to see what patterns of sound, grammar and vocabulary are being used, and in what proportions, and to explain, if possible, why one method of expression has been chosen rather than another, and so on; he is not trying to evaluate the language in terms of some aesthetic, moral, or other critical standard. A linguist may study the language of James Joyce's *Ulysses*, for example, and at the end he will have a very precise knowledge of how Joyce manipulated language to produce the effects he did, but he will not be able to make any decision as to whether *Ulysses* is a good or a bad novel, is pornographic or not, or the characters true-to-life, because these judgements require reference to standards of a non-linguistic nature which the linguist, as linguist, is not professionally competent to set up. Of course, very often the linguist and literary critic are two personae within the one individual: this does not alter the point, which is that two distinct operations are involved in studying an author's language: identifying and describing the salient linguistic features of his utterance, and then evaluating their effect on the reader. And they should not be confused.

Similarly, elocution lessons are not Linguistics. Once again, there is an overlap, of course: both activities are closely connected with the nature of speech sounds, their articulation and reception; but whereas elocution involves studying sounds with the aim of improving their quality in the light of some social or aesthetic standard (i.e. evaluating them), phonetics (that part of Linguistics which studies the basic sounds of speech—see p. 35) investigates all sounds of human speech objectively, whether they conform to any given social or personal standard or not. The short 'a' in 'bath', for example, which is heard in many Northern dialects of English, may be beautiful to some English speakers, and ugly to others (and worth writing to the newspapers about!)—but the phonetician has officially no feelings on the matter. He is only concerned that this sound, as all others, should be given a precise description and definition within a scientific frame of reference. (I shall be describing what this framework is in Chapter 2.)

Fourthly, Linguistics is not to be identified with the older approaches to language study with which most of us are familiar from our early schooldays. There are many ways in which the modern approach to language differs from the 'traditional' approaches, as they are usually called. Traditional grammars, despite many helpful points, are largely remembered for their fundamental misconceptions about the nature of language which they embodied—many of which are regrettably still with us. By discussing briefly the more important of these, I feel we can get a clearer picture of what Linguistics is really about, and why a new approach to language study is so necessary. These misconceptions relate to quite basic issues about language, and few linguists would disagree in their attitude to any of them (though linguists enter into controversy enough in other fields!). They are also the issues which tend to come to the fore in popular discussion, such as in letters to *The Times*. I shall take my examples from English, as this will be the language most familiar to most readers; but what I say about English could also be said about any other modern language which has been studied in traditional terms.

First, in most traditional grammars there is the general absence of any recognition that the spoken and written forms of a language are different media, displaying very different patterns of grammar and vocabulary, and having very different standards of usage. Accordingly, there is a failure to see that the rules made about the one are frequently inapplicable to the other. Rules have been written phrased as if they apply to the entirety of English grammar, whereas in fact they only apply to the written part of it. A rule, for example, which tells us that the regular plural of an English noun is formed by 'adding an *s*', has little counterpart in speech, where there are three quite distinct sounds which we regularly add to nouns to make them plural, depending on the

B

nature of the sound a noun ends with—listen to the endings of the words 'boats', 'trains' and 'horses', where the first sounds like an *s*, the second like a *z*, and the third like the word *is*. Also, rules which instruct us to say 'shall' after 'I' and not 'will', without further qualification, again forget that in speech something very different happens: here, the most frequent form is neither of these, but 'I'll'. Few writers on English have ever bothered to study the spoken language at all, and while this is to a certain extent excusable (tape recorders and similar equipment, prerequisite for any scientific study of speech, are relatively recent inventions), it is none the less the case that to study writing at the expense of speech is to put the cart before the linguistic horse. We need only consider the nature of language briefly to see that this is so. Language, it has been said, is our facility to *talk* to each other. Linguistics does also study writing, but it is important to realise that any written activity is a later and a more sophisticated process than speech. Speech is the primary medium of linguistic expression: we begin to speak before we write, most of us speak far more than we write in everyday life, all natural languages were spoken before they were written, and there are many languages in the world today which have never been written down. To base one's statements about language on writing rather than speech is therefore a reversal of linguistic priorities, and leads to all kinds of confused thinking.

Related to this is the point that in most traditional grammar, the material presented does not even cover the whole range of the language's written forms, but is restricted to specific kinds of writing—the more formal styles, in particular. Anything which smacks of informality tends to be rigorously avoided, or, if included, is castigated as 'slang' and labelled 'Bad Grammar'; though very often the informality is in regular and widespread use by educated people. We do not, after all, use the same kind of formal language when at home or writing a letter to friends as we do when we are giving a speech or applying in writing for a job. A language can be used at many levels of formality, and it should be one of the jobs of a grammar to take account of these differences, and not to select some levels as 'right' and others as 'wrong'. For example, we are all familiar with the 'rule' of English which tells us that we should use 'whom' and not 'who' as relative pronoun in a sentence like 'the man — I saw was tall and dark'. But such rules simply distort the reality of English. It is not a question of 'whom' being correct usage, and 'who' being incorrect: each is correct in certain circumstances and incorrect in others. The difference is essentially one of formality: 'whom' in this context tends to be a more formal way of making the point than 'who', which is more colloquial. It would be inappropriate to introduce formality into an informal, chatty conversation, as it would be to introduce informality into an official occasion. Similarly, compare the sentences 'he removed the chair which I had been sitting on', and 'he removed the chair on which I had been sitting': both are possible in English, and any such rigid statement as *Never end a sentence with a preposition* is consequently unrealistic, as it refuses to take into account the formality differences existing between them.

Again, therefore, from traditional grammar, we tend to get a distorted view of the proportions and function of language forms. We are given the impression that the language described in the grammar books is normal, general usage, whereas in fact it is frequently a specialized variety. There is rarely any explicit reference to the simultaneous existence of different styles of usage in language—that the way in which we speak or write in one situation may be very different from the way we might in another. In language description, absolute standards rarely exist. What we normally refer to as '*the* English language' is in reality, when we examine it, not a single homogeneous thing at all, but a conglomeration of regional and social dialects, or 'sub-languages', all different from each other in various degrees. Probably no two people ever speak in exactly the same way, unless one is deliberately mimicking the other. When we consider factors such as these, we can perhaps see why writing a grammar is so difficult, and why ignorance of stylistic variation in language can be so dangerous.

A second reason for the inadequacy of most traditional grammars is that writers tried to describe English in terms of another language—usually Latin, because of the status which the Classical languages had held as models of description in Europe for centuries. Thus, for example, we find rules about English which tell us to say 'It is I' instead of 'It is me', or tell us that the noun in English has five, or even six cases, namely Nominative ('fish'), Vocative ('O fish'), Accusative ('fish'), Genitive ('of a fish'), Dative ('to/for a fish') and Ablative ('by/with/from a fish'). Now if we examine the situation really carefully, we can see that this is just an attempt to treat English as if it were Latin. And English is *not* Latin. Just because Latin required the nominative case after the verb 'to be' is no reason for concluding that English must also keep the same case for nouns or pronouns in this position. The patterns of English grammar work differently from the patterns of Latin grammar. Similarly, just because Latin had six cases, there is no need to try to force six into English. The procedure gives rise to all kinds of difficulties: for example, 'for the bridge' is called a dative case by traditional grammarians, but 'across the bridge' (which did not simply add an ending in the forms of the noun in Latin) is called a prepositional phrase—even though the two have the same internal structure in English! The mistake is of course to call 'for the bridge' a 'case' of the word 'bridge' in the first place. By the word 'case', grammarians normally refer to one kind of variation in the actual forms of a noun, which shows its relationship to other parts of speech, or its function in the sentence: the variation is called *inflection* and a language which displays it is called an *inflected* language. Latin inflections normally occur at the ends of words, through the addition of suffixes of various kinds. English has hardly any inflectional endings, however, but uses prepositions to produce the same meaning.

To call 'for the bridge' and 'ponti' both dative case is simply to use the one word 'case' in two very different senses. English has in fact only two noun cases: the genitive case (where we add an *s*-like sound, as in *cat's, boys', horse's*) and a general case which is used everywhere else—*boy, boys*. To think otherwise is an obvious example of Latin interfering with our description of English, and in a way it is rather laughable (when one thinks of 'O fish', for instance). But there are far less obvious cases of misrepresentation in English for the same reason—the insistence, for example, that English has the same range of tenses as Latin— and these are more serious precisely because we tend to overlook them.

The general point to be made, therefore, is that in the description of a language, or some part of a language, we must not impose findings from the description of some other language— even if we have a strong preference for this other language. English must be described in its own terms, and not through Latin spectacles. English is a complex enough language without trying to force the complexities of Latin into it. This is not of course to deny the existence of genuine points of similarity between any two languages; but such points must always be taken as hypotheses which have to be carefully tested. And this is one of the things which the linguist does.

In traditional grammars, then, there is a tendency to treat Latin as a kind of authority which one can turn to when wondering what to do about English grammar. There are, however, other authorities invoked in grammars of this kind, or in everyday conversation about language, which produce equally unrealistic results. For instance, people often appeal to a criterion of logic of some sort, when making statements about the way a language is constructed. One often hears things like 'English is a more logical language than French' or 'It's much more logical to say *spoonfuls* than *spoonsful*'. Statements of this kind confuse two standards of usage which should be kept quite apart, the standard of linguistic usage, and that of logical usage. Human language is not a logical construct, though some people would have it so; it is not beautifully regular. It can change its form, sometimes quite unpredictably, over the years, and it is full of irregularities. One cannot apply logical reasoning to language: we say 'big-bigger' and 'small-smaller', but if we adopt a logical position then we should be forced to say that 'good-gooder' is the correct form; and I doubt whether there is anyone who would seriously want to defend this. Again, to insist that 'two negatives in English make a positive' is also to land oneself in theoretical difficulties: sometimes two negatives do logically make a positive (for example, 'I am not dissatisfied' is almost synonymous with 'I am satisfied'—though never *exactly* the same), but very often two negatives go together to make a more emphatic negative—the little boy who says 'I've not done nothing' being a case in point. Here he does not mean 'I have done something'! We may not like his way of putting it, and call it 'sub-standard' usage, or 'bad' grammar, but we should note that the source of any objection is that we do not like the dialect he is using; it is not a logical question at all. In short, it is best in language matters not to mention the word 'logic', but to talk instead in terms of 'regular' and 'irregular' forms, and to show how there is always a tendency for the irregular forms in language to be made to conform to the pattern of the regular ones—a process which we refer to as *analogy*. The best examples of analogy are always to be found in the speech of children who are learning to speak: the child who says 'mouses' or 'I seed' for 'mice' and 'I saw' is simply treating irregular forms as if they were regular ones.

There is no 'most logical' language. Nor, similarly, is there a 'most complex' language, where complexity means 'difficult to learn'. Standards of difficulty are relative: a thing is more difficult to do depending on how much practice we have had at doing it, and how used we are to doing similar things. If someone says that 'Russian must be an awfully difficult language to learn', this may be true, for that person, but we must be careful not to draw the conclusion that 'Russian is therefore a difficult language'. Whether it is hard to learn depends in particular on whether one speaks a language which is at all similar to Russian in its sounds, grammar and vocabulary. If one does, then Russian will be a lot easier to learn than for one who does not. On the whole, the greater the grammatical and other differences between one's own language and any other, the more difficult (or 'complex', if you prefer) will that language turn out to be. But Russian is not, absolutely speaking, a more difficult language than English: a Russian, after all, finds learning English just as difficult.

Similarly, we must not talk about some languages as if they were 'simple', 'crude' or 'primitive' languages. This often happens when we talk about the languages of tribes in Africa or South America which are said to be at a very low level of cultural development. But just because a tribe happens to be, anthropologically speaking, 'primitive' is no reason to argue that its language is linguistically speaking 'primitive', for it never is. The word 'primitive' implies being near the bottom of a scale or standard of development of some kind; and while such standards may exist in comparative anthropology, they have not been shown to exist in language. As we have already seen, the only realistic standard we ought to apply to a language is the language itself: we cannot measure one language against the yardstick provided by another. Now just because some tribe does not have as many words as English, let us say, it does not follow that it is 'more primitive' than English. It has no need of so many words, that is all. It has enough words for its own purposes: the people do not require the vast range of technical terms which English has, for example. And if the tribe, through some process of economic development, did begin to come into contact with technical things, then new words would be coined or borrowed, so that people could cope. It is ridiculous to think that a language could exist where there were insufficient words for the people to talk about any aspect of their environment they wished. Language always keeps pace with the social development of its users. And an argument about primitiveness always cuts both ways: what a tribal language may lack in technical terms it makes up for by probably being better equipped than English to talk about different kinds of jungle fruit, for example. We should thus be able to see that such old arguments as 'the French have a word for it' (implying, presumably, that in this respect French is a better language than one's own) are not valid. It might take the English language ten or a hundred words to talk about a notion that French expresses in one, but we can still talk about this notion to our own satisfaction. And similarly, there are many English concepts which do not exist in single words in French. Languages are not better or worse; only different; but people do continue to talk as if there were a perennial linguistic Derby which they had a vested interest in!

Logic and complexity are two standards frequently appealed to in arguments about the nature of language. Another standard is the aesthetic one: a language, word, structure or sound, is said to be more 'beautiful', 'ugly', 'affected', and so on, than another. This was a very common attitude in older times, when beauty was frequently associated with eloquence and the Classics. Thomas Elyot's remark, written in 1570, sums up the dominant attitude of an age: 'the providence of God hath left unto us in no other tongue save only in the Greek and Latin tongue, the true precepts and the perfect examples of eloquence'. At this time, Spanish and French were viewed as examples of 'much decayed' Latin, and grammar throughout most of the late Middle Ages was 'the art of speaking and writing *well*'—and the nearer to Cicero one could get, the better! These days, aesthetic judgements about language are particularly common when talking about people's accents, or ways of pronunciation, and again it is an unrealistic standard. No one sound is intrinsically better or more beautiful than another. We respond to other people's language in terms of our own social background and familiarity with their speech. If we are from Liverpool, then Liverpudlian speech will sound more 'pleasant' than if we are not. This is simply one of the sociolinguistic facts of life. If we insist on criticizing someone else's accent as 'affected' or 'ugly'. or some other adjective—for example, 'I find Cockney speech so harsh and unmusical, don't you?'—then we are simply trying to impose our own standards of beauty onto others, judging other people in terms of our own particular linguistic preferences. We usually forget that we probably sound just as odd to the person we are criticizing. Of course, some accents are from the point of view of society more useful or influential than others. A strong rural accent is frequently not acceptable in many city jobs, and a city accent equally unacceptable in the country. But this is a different matter, and is not primarily a question of aesthetic standards at all.

Yet a fourth authority people constantly turn to is history. Here the argument is that the 'true' or 'correct' meaning of a word is its oldest one. Thus, the real meaning of 'history', it might be argued, is 'investigation', because this was the meaning of *historia* in Greek; or the real meaning of 'nice' is 'fastidious', as this was one of the senses it had in Shakespeare's time. Frequently, indeed, people go so far as to call a word 'meaningless' because it no longer has a particular earlier meaning—'nice' being a case in point. But this ultra-conservative point of view is reducible to absurdity, and illustrates another confusion of two sets of criteria which should be kept apart. This time the confusion is between the historical and non-historical dimensions of study. The meaning of a modern English word is to be found (and can only be found) by studying the way in which the word is used *in modern English*—the kinds of object or idea currently being referred to. The meanings a word may have had years ago are irrelevant to this. We do not criticize modern English trousers by reference to Greek or Elizabethan ideals. Why then should we criticize our modern linguistic habits for not living up to older standards?

We can easily show the absurdity of this reliance on history in discussing meaning—the 'etymological fallacy' it is sometimes

called—by following the reasoning to its logical conclusion. If
the oldest meaning of a word is the correct one, then we can
hardly stop with Shakespeare! We must trace the meaning of
'nice', for example, back into Old French (where the word *nice*
meant 'silly') and thence to Latin (where *nescius* meant 'ignorant')
and thence to the ancestor language of Latin, where it had a
meaning that no one is really very clear about. And of course
even this is not the 'oldest' language: the oldest language is
unattainable, lost for ever, never written down, and thus without
records. So on the above argument, we shall *never* know the
real meaning of the words we use. But if we never know the
meaning of words, how can we use them to talk to each other?
The falsity of the argument should be transparent. Far better to
accept the fact of language change, in sounds, grammar and
vocabulary, and treat each new linguistic generation afresh, in its
own terms.

A particular aspect of this confusion of historical and non-
historical criteria is quite common in traditional grammar
books, as well as in everyday arguments about the meaning of
words. This is the way in which grammarians, writing about
modern English let us say, frequently spend a great deal of time
talking about the older states of the language in their books, or
have recourse to the older forms of English in order to explain
the modern ones. An example of the former would be a grammarian who begins to tell you about the verb in modern English
by explaining how many classes of verbs there were in Anglo-
Saxon, or who tells you that one of the interjections in English is
'forsooth'. It should not be necessary to comment on this kind
of thing. An example of the latter would be the grammarian
who insists on describing the auxiliary verb 'ought' as if it were
the past tense of 'owe'—this used to be the case, but no longer is.
Such reasoning is irrelevant to the study of modern English:
there is enough to be said about the use of 'ought' without
going into the uses it once had. One does not need past information to study the present state of a language. And the reverse,

incidentally, is also true: to read modern English structure into a study of Anglo-Saxon can be equally distorting.

The mention of Shakespeare a page ago brings to mind a fifth authority which grammarians and others like to turn to, namely, the usage of the 'best' authors. Early dictionaries did this also, including only those words which had been used by a reputable author. Most of the quotations illustrating grammatical rules in even fairly modern grammatical handbooks are taken from famous novelists or non-fiction writers. Clearly, the result of applying such a standard is to produce a description of a very restricted, specialized, literary English. If we all spoke like Jane Austen all the time, as many grammar books it seems would have us do, the result would be intolerable! But it is not only the grammarian who takes this line. We frequently find in popular discussion slogans like 'Preserve the tongue which Shakespeare spoke!'— this particular one was recently used by the headmaster of a well-known school in a newspaper article. The English language is held to have 'decayed' since this period of literary excellence— which is simply another instance of the view that all change in language is for the worse, and that the older states of a language are intrinsically superior to the more recent. This view we have already had cause to criticize in the preceding two paragraphs.

A sixth authority frequently invoked by a grammarian— perhaps the most frequent of all—is himself, though he does not usually admit it. Many textbooks are clearly impressionistic at many points, rules being based on a half-baked awareness of the author's own usage. It is in fact extremely difficult to write even a part of a grammar of a language based upon oneself as the 'informant', the source of information about what is going on. Very often—much more often than one might think—people make statements about their own speech which are utterly wrong. For example, many seem convinced that they speak 'too quickly' (whereas what they are referring to is normal conversational speed), that their usual pronunciation of words like 'him' and 'her' includes a 'h' sound (whereas these words rarely do unless spoken in isolation or with a strong stress), and so on. And a similar ignorance is usually at the basis of an Englishman's criticism of 'Americanisms' in others' speech, where what is being attacked is normally *any* usage which does not conform to his own feeling about what is 'proper' English, whether it stems from America or not. Few people know exactly which parts of the language have been directly influenced by American usage, and unfortunately they tend to use the label 'Americanism' as a general term of abuse.

At other times, it is difficult or impossible to be sure what one actually does say. This is particularly the case if there is any divided usage in the community at large. For example, do you say, or would you find acceptable, such sentences as: 'He is regarded insane', 'I was sat opposite by a stranger', 'John and Mary aren't very loved', 'That baby is silly and crying'? Very often, you simply cannot be sure. It is a temptation to take a first impression as being the truth, and this is very dangerous. A person may even feel absolutely certain about the way he says something (for example, that he pronounces '*con*troversy' with the main stress on the first syllable), and then a few days (or even minutes) later he may catch himself saying 'con*tro*versy', with the stress on the second. And if there are such problems over an individual's own usage, how much more is there a problem over determining the usage of others. Language is filled with questions of acceptability, and each descriptive statement a grammarian makes must be thoroughly tested by supplementing his own intuition with information derived from other people's intuitions about their language. And if it is the case that 50 people say one thing and 50 people say another, then this division in usage must be reflected in the rules about pronunciation or grammar. It is not a question of one being right and the other wrong: as we have seen, both are, to a certain degree, acceptable.

Another aspect of an impressionistic approach to linguistic description is that the information which ultimately appears in a grammar book is highly selective. No traditional grammar is anywhere near complete, that is, providing a complete description of all the sentences of the language. No linguistically-based grammar is near completion either, come to that, but at least the linguist is more aware of exactly what has not been done, and does not act as if his partial description were a whole one. A grammar should contain rules which will account for *all* the structures in current use, the exceptions as well as the regularities.

We could spend a whole textbook talking about these inadequacies of the traditional approaches to language that the linguist is so dissatisfied with; but we shall just mention one more before passing on to other matters. This is not so much a question of authority or usage as of methodology. Traditional grammar is characterized by extreme vagueness of definition, and a failure to be explicit about important issues. Often crucial (and questionable) theoretical assumptions about the language or the grammar are made but not stated explicitly, and many terms needed to talk about language are badly defined. The clearest example of badly defined terms is that of the parts of speech. Parts of speech are supposed to tell us something about how the grammar of a language works. Everyone will agree about this. But the traditional definitions of many of the parts of speech are usually most ungrammatical. The noun, for example, is regularly defined as being 'the name of a person, place or thing'. But this definition tells us nothing about the *grammar* of nouns at all; it merely gives us a rather vague indication of what nouns are used to refer to in the outside world—what they mean. A grammatical definition of 'noun' must give us grammatical information: it should, for example, tell us where in a sentence nouns can appear, how they inflect, whether they follow or precede articles and prepositions, and so on. The above definition gives us none of this. Moreover, the information which it does give, apart from its irrelevance, is so vague as to be useless. Are abstract nouns like 'beauty' included in the definition? Can one reasonably say that 'beauty' is a thing? Similarly, if verbs are defined as 'doing words', then what about words like 'seem' and 'be', which are definitely verbs, but which *do* nothing? And what about those nouns which refer to actions, like 'breathing' (in 'His breathing was irregular') or 'punch' (in 'He gave him a punch')? On the basis of their meaning, these words could equally well be called verbs or nouns, being just as much 'doing' words as 'thing' words.

We can see, through examples such as this, that defining parts of speech in terms of their meaning is yet another case of the intrusion of irrelevant factors into grammatical study. Moreover, it is not only the parts of speech which are affected in this way. Consider one of the traditional definitions of the sentence in this light: 'the sentence expresses a complete thought'. It is hardly helpful information for the student wanting to learn a new language (that is, wanting to learn how to use the sentences of that language) to be told that sentences express thoughts, and, moreover, complete ones, whatever *they* are! In any case, he probably knew this already, as sentences surely express thoughts in all languages. In short, rules of grammar should not be based on the meaning of the forms in question (and by 'forms' here I mean any isolatable bit of language, like a word, a clause, a sentence, or a part of any of these), but on the way these forms behave in relation to other forms in the language as a whole, so as to produce predictable, characteristic patterns. Questions of defining the meaning of these forms can be left until one has first got a good idea in one's mind as to exactly what these forms are.

The word most frequently used to sum up the traditional attitude to language is 'prescriptive': writers were concerned to make rules about how people *ought* to speak and write, in conformity with some standard they held dear. They were not concerned with ascertaining first how people actually *did* speak and write. But before one can prescribe rules about language, one must first describe the facts about the language. This is really the central difference between the new and the old attitudes to language, the difference between Linguistics and traditional grammar. Modern linguists want to describe language in its own terms; they do not want to gear their description to non-linguistic standards of correctness. A linguist is aware that the grammarian of a language does not 'make' the rules of that language. A grammarian cannot do this, and he should not. He should restrict his ambitions to codifying what is already there, the usage of the people who speak the language. If a grammarian attempts to overreach himself, he will lose: his rules will be overruled by the weight of majority usage, if this differs from what he prescribes, and people will ignore his prescriptions when using their language unselfconsciously. This situation has in fact developed in English. People do not speak in accordance with the rules of traditional grammar books, and are aware of this. The unfortunate thing, of course, is that many who do perceive this difference allow themselves to be worried by it. They very often try to speak 'grammatically', or tell their children to—that is, attempt to conform to a rule that some scholar thought up years before which no longer has any general force in English. What they do not realize is that they speak grammatically already, and that their usage has in fact a greater authority than the old grammars' rules because their usage is alive whereas that of the grammar books is fossilized. This is a point we have got to remember. Language is always changing. A grammar book, once in print, does not change. *Ergo*, in the nature of things, a grammar book is always a little or a lot behind the times. All books describing the present states of languages, whether their pronunciation, grammar or vocabulary, have to be brought up to date every few years if they are to stay realistic. Thus an identical argument to the above could be used about dictionaries, which should similarly be thought of not as authorities which tell us how we must use words, but as sources of information about how words are used. *We* tell the lexicographer what to put in the dictionary, and not the other way round.

To a linguist, then, of two alternative usages, one is not 'right' and the other 'wrong'—the two are merely different. He must describe both in his study, and leave others to decide which is socially more appropriate to which situations. Thus, comparing the sentences 'The man whom I saw was your uncle' and 'The man who I saw was your uncle', he does not say that 'whom' is right and 'who' is wrong, or vice versa. He says that in the English of educated people either may occur, but that 'whom' is more appropriate for formal contexts, and 'who' for the more colloquial. The word 'appropriate' is a much better word to use in this connection than the word 'correct'. One of the linguist's tasks is to attack the naïve, egocentric purism which colours so many judgements about language, and which wastes so many people's time and money. Most of the letters about language written to the daily or weekly press (B.B.C. announcers are particularly prone to attack) could have been saved if people were made to realize fully the fact of language change and its implications. More seriously, careers can be in danger if employers or examiners act through ignorance, and react against a person on account of his manner of speaking or writing, or his attitude towards language. There are cases on record of people being sacked because of their accent.

Authorities now seem to be getting more aware of dangers of this kind, though the awareness has not really percolated through all levels of education. A recent enlightened statement can be found in a Secondary Schools Examination Council paper for the Department of Education and Science called *The examining of the English language*.[1] In talking about the Ordinary Level English language examinations, they say: 'Another criticism we have of these questions is that they frequently require candidates to give judgements on the "correctness" of a particular usage without reference to its context. Candidates are given no opportunity to consider in what circumstances the usage might be appropriate. It is wrong to assume that there is only one correct answer to these questions . . .; the examinations suffer from an assumption that there is a universal standard of correctness appropriate to all contexts. In the

[1] H.M.S.O., 1964, by permission of the Controller; Crown copyright reserved.

examinations there are as yet few signs of concern for the continuing development of the language, or for the fact that different modes of expression are appropriate to different situations' (p. 13). The authors of the paper point to the large amount of time spent preparing students to answer these questions in the required way, even though this preparation has little value in developing powers of expression, and conclude that 'the main source of the trouble is that many teachers, and many examiners, who are drawn from the ranks of teachers, have hitherto not been equipped by their training or subsequent experience with the elements of an effective and systematic approach to the study of the English language. They therefore tend to apply over-simplified and misleading rules' (p. 13). The paper ends with a number of recommendations, the final one being particularly relevant for this book: 'We should also like to see the foundations laid for a study of some of the basic principles of Linguistics, with English as the language of exemplification' (p. 30).

I too should like to see this, but this chapter should make it clear that the climate of the time is not quite ready for it. There is still a great deal of groundwork to be done, both in terms of puncturing the complacency about language which already exists, and in terms of providing people with something which they can put in its place. We must now go on to look at some aspects of the alternative approach to language study which Linguistics proposes, and begin to be a little more constructive.

CHAPTER TWO

What Linguistics Is

So far, I have been approaching Linguistics largely by discussing what the subject is *not* concerned with, an unfortunately necessary step at the present time. But in so doing I have had to make some reference on a number of occasions to what linguists do in fact do. It may be useful to recapitulate these points before going on to amplify them. It should be clear from Chapter 1, then, that Linguistics performs at least two tasks: it is concerned with the study of particular languages as ends in themselves, in order to be able to produce complete and accurate descriptions of them; and it also studies languages as a means to a further end, in order to be able to obtain information about the nature of language in general. The linguist is thus one who wants to find out how language 'works', and he does this through the study of specific languages. He tries to be as objective as possible, and aims to avoid the misconceptions about the nature of language and languages which have been so dominant. He therefore focuses his attention on the speech-habits of a community, only secondarily on the writing-habits (unless of course the language only exists in a written form, like Classical Hebrew). He tries to describe each language in its own terms—not reading in considerations which are applicable only to some other language—and all styles, or levels of usage of that language, not just concentrating on literary or formal styles. He endeavours to keep his criteria of description linguistic, that is, arising solely out of the nature of language, and does not introduce criteria from other aspects of human behaviour, such as standards of logic, aesthetics, or literary excellence, to explain points of usage.

He keeps clear in his mind the distinction between historical and non-historical information, and does not allow irrelevant information about past usage to colour his assessment of any one state of a language. He avoids being prescriptive. He avoids making careless, impressionistic judgements about what he thinks happens in language, and takes account of the usage of the native-speakers of the language he is investigating. He tries to systematize his observations about a language by relating them all to a linguistic theory devised for the purpose. And he tries to go beyond the superficial aspects of language structure to see what the really important forces operating on and within the language are. This, one might argue, is the behaviour of the 'compleat linguist'.

Put simply, Linguistics is the scientific way of studying language—or perhaps it should be Language, to emphasize the fact that we mean both language in general as well as languages in particular. This definition now requires us to examine the implications of its two central words, 'scientific' and 'language'. First of all, then, 'scientific'. This is best explained by a very quick look at the history of language study. People have of course been interested in the nature of language for years. If we go back as far as we can in studying the history of a community, we usually find evidence of a conscious or unconscious awareness of the importance or intrinsic potential of language. We can see this, for example, in the way in which different cultures link the origin of speech and writing with magic or religion, or find in language mystical processes of various kinds. But we can also see a scholarly interest in language from the earliest period of recorded history. We find discussion of fundamental issues connected with language throughout the periods of Classical Greece and Rome, beginning with Plato in the fourth century B.C., and continuing in the work of Aristotle, the Stoics, Cicero, Varro, Priscian, and many others—even Julius Caesar wrote something on grammar. It also appears in very early Indian civilization, again tied to religion. Linguistic interest is in evidence throughout the Middle Ages in Europe: we see it in the writing of many Arabic scholars in the ninth and tenth centuries, throughout the whole period of the Renaissance, and it continues right through until the nineteenth century, when historical studies of language began to take a new tack.

But while there has been a strong interest in language all this time, and while modern Linguistics is certainly indebted to much of this early work and has borrowed from it, there are a number of crucial differences between the modern state of the subject and this older study of language. The central difference is that this older study was not, in a word, scientific; that is, it lacked the characteristics which we would nowadays associate with a science. These characteristics are not simply reducible to modern machines and abstract symbols: Linguistics can display these a-plenty, with its electronic equipment for speech analysis and synthesis, and the symbology it is developing to talk about grammar, which at times seems to have been lifted straight out of an algebra handbook. And it is true that working in a Linguistics department in a university these days, one may find people with a degree in logic, mathematics or electrical engineering, as well as others with one in English, Classics or Modern Languages. But this is the more superficial side to the scientific-ness of Linguistics. More important is the way the subject relies on scientific techniques, especially on a 'scientific method'. Observation of events prior to the setting-up of a hypothesis, which is then systematically investigated via experimentation and a theory developed—this is standard procedure in Linguistics as in other sciences. Also in common is the concern to establish sound theoretical principles and a clear and consistent termin-ology. Again, in the older period, Linguistics lacked autonomy: study of language was usually subservient to the requirements of such other studies as logic, rhetoric, philosophy, history or literary criticism. It was an amateur's field; and scholars often investigated language haphazardly, selecting different aspects for study merely on grounds of interest, and often carrying a line of linguistic reasoning too far, to support a particular, non-linguistic point of view. Many bitter controversies, such as how language first developed in human beings, or whether Hebrew was in truth the oldest language in the world, would now find no place at all in Linguistics. The twentieth century has changed the whole basis and framework of language study; and it is this central, total shift in attitude which is at the bottom of the term 'scientific'.

We must now have a look at just what we mean by 'language', the other unknown in our definition. What is involved in studying a language scientifically? This is a question which cannot be answered in one sentence, or even a paragraph, although people regularly try to sum language up in a few words. It is such a familiar phenomenon that we can very easily fall into the trap of thinking that we know all about it. 'Of course I know what language is', someone might say, 'I use it all the time, don't I?' Or again, '*Everyone* knows what language is, so why make such a song and dance over it?' But this is to be fooled by our upbringing; it is a contempt bred by our familiarity with language. We do not remember the long period of trial and error which accompanies the learning of our mother-tongue. Language, like all other skills, does not come naturally; we have to be taught how to use it. Once it has been learned, we tend to take it for granted —until, of course, something starts to go wrong, or we find we have to make an abnormal use of it. It is when we are asked to provide therapy for a child with a speech defect, or required to learn a new language, or find we have to write something for a public to read, that we begin to realize the complexity of what we have mastered. In the case of language, too, we can afford to be complacent even less than with other skills, in view of the ambiguity inherent in the word. The *O.E.D.* lists over a dozen distinct senses of 'language', and it is chastening to look these up. We then very quickly find that we do not have an instinctive knowledge of what language is, that there is much more to it than meets the eye or ear, that people do *not* all mean the same

What is Linguistics?

thing by the word 'language', and that this disparity is sometimes at the bottom of many arguments.

Language, to put it mildly, is a very complex phenomenon; there is too much going on for it all to be summed up or dismissed in a few general statements. To begin with, there is both a functional side to language—the jobs language does in human society—and there is a formal side—the way language is structured. I shall not try to give either a functional or a formal definition of language here, because it would take a long time to explain the terms in such definitions satisfactorily. But I shall suggest some of the central features of language which anyone seriously trying to frame a definition would have to bear in mind.

First of all, let us look at what is involved in an approach to language which begins by considering its function. What is language's main job? The answer is clear: language is the most frequently used and most highly developed form of human communication. The implications of this statement are very interesting. An act of communication is basically the transmission of information of some kind—a 'message'—from a source to a receiver. In the case of language, both source and receiver are human, and the message is transmitted either vocally, through the air, or graphically, by marks on a surface, usually paper. Language is one form of communication. There are of course others, not necessarily connected with human behaviour; for example, the instinctive noises which animals of a given species use to communicate with each other. This is communication, as language is, but there is little in common between human and animal forms of communication. And if one insists on talking about the 'language' of the birds and bees then one must remember that this is a different, and strictly analogical sense of the word 'language'. What the linguist means by language is essentially a human phenomenon. He would also refrain from using the word 'language' to refer to metaphorical senses of communication: for instance, when one says that a bond of communication exists between musicians, conductor and composer, so that all three 'speak the same language'.

But even if one restricts the term 'language' to human communication, it is still the case that not everything which would fall under this heading is language, in the linguist's sense. We can see the reason for this if we consider all the other possibilities of human communication. We may communicate with our mouths, or with other parts of our face, or indeed by making use of any of our senses. Only the visual and vocal/auditory senses are frequently used, but there is nothing to stop us using other methods if we find them appropriate to our purpose. Some secret societies have a system of communication by touch, and one occasionally comes across advertisements which have the scent of the product they display impregnating the paper. But on the whole the use of the senses of taste, touch and smell are extremely restricted as far as human communication is concerned.

The visual system, however, is well-established in human beings: we need only think of all the facial expressions and bodily gestures we make use of in our day-to-day activity—hand-signals, winks, raised eyebrows, and so on—which communicate a great deal of information. Often, we pay more attention to the way a person looks than the way he speaks—'the expression on his face told me he was lying', a novelist might say, or 'it wasn't so much what he said as the way he looked when he said it'. And we are all familiar with the kinds of ambiguity which arise when we cannot see the person we are speaking or listening to—in a telephone conversation, for example, or when watching television with the picture temporarily missing. But despite its importance, the visual system of communication in humans does not have by any means the same structure as the vocal—there is nothing really like grammar, for instance—and the linguist does not therefore call it language. He restricts the term 'language' yet further to a *vocal* system of human communication. He only allows the visual a place in language in the single instance of writing, which differs from other visual communicative activity in that it is usually an attempt to directly transcribe our speech in a one-to-one way. All modern writing-systems are designed to copy speech, to turn sounds into letters, thereby making our message more permanent; other visual signs do not do this. Finally, in discussing human communicational activity other than language, we must mention those noises which a human being can produce other than from his mouth, which can communicate information; an example would be finger-snapping. These too the linguist would exclude in his attempt to make the notion of language precise.

But there are still other restrictions which we must place on the term 'language'. So far we have called it a system of human vocal communication. But even here, not all of this is linguistic. There are many sounds, or aspects of sounds, which we utter that are not linguistic, that is, we cannot or do not deliberately make use of them in order to communicate a message. For example, a sneeze, a snore, or our breathing are audible vocal noises which do not communicate a message in the same sense as when we speak words or sentences. A sneeze may communicate the fact that we have a cold, of course, but this is a very different sense of the word 'communication'. It is communication 'despite oneself'. It directly reflects a particular physiological state on our part, and has no meaning other than this. Words, on the other hand, are not tied down to our bodily state: we may speak or not speak (but we have no similar option in breathing or snoring), and we may use a particular word whenever we wish, regardless of the physical state we happen to be in (but we cannot sneeze at will). Uncontrolled or uncontrollable vocal noises of this type, lacking any clear internal structure or conventional meaning, are not part of language.

Another set of vocal effects which we would exclude from language is that commonly referred to by the label 'voice quality'. While we speak, apart from the actual message we are trying to put across, we also communicate information of a quite different kind, operating at an entirely different level. This is information about our personalities. Whenever we speak, we make known our identity to the outside world; there are features of everyone's voice which allow others to recognize an individual without seeing him. These features are difficult to pin down precisely, but they clearly exist, and they are very different from the rest of our utterance. Voice quality is a relatively permanent feature of our speech; it only alters with age or physiological change (as when one develops a hoarse throat, for instance). Mimics (people who deliberately imitate another's voice quality) are the exception in society rather than the rule. Normally, people can do nothing about their voice quality, nor do they usually *want* to change it—unless they have some professional interest in mimicry or acting. Similarly, in writing: a person's handwriting is the factor which allows us to recognize anyone for who he is, and we only alter this on very exceptional occasions.

To exclude voice quality from language is not thereby to exclude 'accent', of course. 'Accent' is a more general phenomenon, which can be used to refer to the *totality* of sonic features a person has (including his voice quality), but which is usually restricted to the non-idiosyncratic features of his pronunciation —that is, to those sounds which would also be used by a number of other people and which inform us that someone comes from a particular region or social group. Voice quality tells us who someone is, accent where he is from.

Idiosyncratic facets of vocal communication are not to be considered as language. Language, we have implied, is essentially a controlled behaviour, *shared* in various degrees by all the people in a given speech-community. Language transcends idiosyncrasy. Unless we all shared basically the same set of vocal conventions, we would not be able to communicate with each other. It is true that no two people ever speak exactly alike all the time; but the difference between speakers of the same language are *far* outweighed by the similarities. Society does not tolerate too much idiosyncrasy, too much originality, in language. The person who deviates too markedly from the standard forms of the language in an idiosyncratic way is either hailed as a great poet or classified as belonging to one of a very small number of categories, e.g. someone with a speech disorder, an uneducated foreigner, a lunatic.

We began by looking at the central function of language, and in developing this point we have been able to characterize language by reference to a number of factors. We may now summarize the discussion so far by referring to language as human vocal noise (or the graphic representation of this noise in writing) used systematically and conventionally by a community for purposes of communication. Occasionally, language is used for purposes other than communication—for example, to let off steam (as in one's vocal reaction to hitting a finger with a hammer), or to give delight to oneself purely because of the sonic effect which language has upon the ear (as in children's word-play), or as a vehicle for one's own thoughts when no one else is present. But such uses of language are very secondary.

We must now go on to amplify the phrase 'vocal noise' used in the previous paragraph, and in doing so, we shall move from a functional to a formal view of language. The question is now: What is the structure of language? It is a question which still creates a great deal of controversy among certain linguists; but everyone is at least agreed that language does have a structure, and there are a number of features of this structure which people rarely quibble about. In order to discuss any of these features, however, it is necessary to look at language as if it were an artefact, which could be broken down into various components. Whenever we use language in real life, of course, all these components occur simultaneously, but when seen thus, it is an impossibly complex phenomenon to analyse. In order to make any sense out of language at all, we must cut it up into bits, and examine each in turn. But we must never forget that these bits are the linguist's constructs; that what we are doing is trying to build a model, or image, of language in order to be able to explain it and say illuminating things about it. We must also remember that there are many ways of describing the structure of an object: the one outlined here must not be taken as being the *only* method of doing things. It is easy to get this impression from an introductory book on a subject, which has to concentrate on one viewpoint for reasons of space and clarity; and I am anxious that people should not consider the following approach as being in any sense *ex cathedra*. It is simply one view of language which I have found particularly helpful in teaching this subject.

We can first of all look at language by seeing it from the point of view of its actual method of articulation in human beings, and the physical substance out of which it is constituted. The study of the vocal organs, through which we pronounce the basic sounds of speech, the study of sound waves, which is the way sounds are transmitted through the air from one person to another, and the study of the way in which human beings perceive sounds are three interdependent aspects of a single branch of Linguistics which goes under the separate name of *phonetics*. Phonetics is thus the science of human speech-sounds; it studies the defining characteristics of *all* human vocal noise, and concentrates its attention on those sounds which occur in the world's languages. It teaches people to recognize the different sounds which occur in the spoken form of any language, and moreover to produce them for themselves. It trains people to describe the many ways in which the tongue, lips, and other vocal organs function in order to produce these sounds; and it also provides training in methods of finding out about their physical characteristics, using various machines such as the oscillograph and spectrograph—this latter aspect usually being referred to as *acoustic* phonetics. A man who specializes in studying the phonetic features of language is called a phonetician.

We can illustrate one of the ways in which phonetics describes speech by considering some of the sounds we can make using the very front of the mouth, the lips and teeth in particular. First of all, we can articulate sounds using both lips: such sounds are described as *bilabial*. If we observe languages carefully, we can find three types of bilabial consonant, differing in the manner in which they are pronounced. First, we may press the lips tightly together, allowing air from the lungs to build up behind them, and then release the air suddenly, to produce an explosive effect: examples of these sounds, known as *plosives*, would be the [p] sound as in English *pit* and the [b] sound of *bit*. We should in passing note the important differences between these two sounds: the first is pronounced with the lips quite tense, with a puff of air (*aspiration*) upon release of the lips, and with the vocal cords not vibrating; the second is pronounced with the lips more relaxed, with no aspiration, and with the vocal cords vibrating. Differences of this kind are usually summed up using a single pair of labels, *voiceless* and *voiced*: [p] is a voiceless bilabial plosive, [b] is a voiced bilabial plosive. The square brackets used in phonetics help to show that we are talking about sounds and not about the letters of the everyday alphabet. In this particular case, we use the same symbols for [p] and [b] as are used in normal English orthography; but as we shall see, this does not always happen.

The second kind of articulation using both lips takes place by pressing the lips firmly together, as for plosive sounds, but allowing the air to come out through the nose in a continuous stream: this produces a *nasal* sound, which may be both voiceless [m̥] (as in the Welsh word *mhen*, 'my head') or voiced [m] (as in English *mat*). Third, we can put the lips very closely together, but not pressed tight, and produce a continuous hissing noise: such sounds are referred to as *fricatives* (because of the friction which we can hear during their articulation). Bilabial fricatives would be written down with the symbols [φ] and [β] for voiceless and voiced sounds respectively, in the most widely used system of phonetic notation that we have (that of the International Phonetic Association): we can find examples of the former in Japanese or German, of the latter in Spanish.

Plosives, nasals and fricatives may of course occur in other parts of the mouth, along with further types of articulation which we shall not be illustrating here. For example, if we look at the range of sounds which is pronounced when the bottom lip is placed against the top teeth (*labio-dental* sounds), we find more fricatives ([f] and [v] as in English *fat* and *vat*, for example) and nasals (such as [ɱ], which may be heard to occur in a word like English *comfort*, where, because the [m] precedes an [f] sound, its place of articulation is slightly changed). And if we listen to the sounds we can make with the tongue against the teeth (*dental* sounds), we find plosives [t̪] and [d̪], such as occur in French. (These are slightly different from the [t] and [d] of English, which are generally pronounced with the tip of the tongue against the gum behind the top teeth, and not against the teeth themselves.) We would also find fricatives [θ] and [ð], as in English *thin* and *this* respectively. All these sounds are quite easy to distinguish, largely because we can feel the movements of the vocal organs very clearly, and indeed see much of what is going on if we care to look in a mirror. The further back in the mouth we go, however, the more difficult it becomes to sense changes in our articulation, and the more we need training in order to be able to understand what is going on. It may come as a surprise to learn that the initial consonants in English *keep* and *car* are articulated in quite different positions, the tongue touching the roof of the mouth further forward in the first [k] sound than in the second. And there are many other sounds equally difficult to distinguish.

This is no place to embark on a description of the entire range of sounds the human being can articulate: the interested reader can obtain further information on this point by consulting the books in Appendix A. It should be sufficiently clear from what has been said that phonetics is concerned to establish precisely what goes on when one speaks, either in the mouth (as in the above instances of articulatory phonetic analysis), or in the air (as in acoustic phonetics), or in the ear (as in auditory phonetics). We have also seen that one of its important tasks is devising a means of writing down all speech sounds (a *phonetic transcription*) in order to be able to make a permanent and unambiguous record of what goes on in speech. Our usual alphabets, which we use for everyday writing, are not sufficient to do this task precisely: there are, after all, only twenty-six basic letter types in our English alphabet, but there are over forty basic sounds. We all know how English tries to get round this problem: it uses the same letter or letters for different sounds, as in the many ways in which the *ough* combination can be pronounced, and it gives the same sound all sorts of different spellings: the same vowel [i] appears in *sit, women, village, busy* and *enough*, for example. This method is both uneconomical (two or more letters for one sound), and, more important, highly ambiguous: one cannot predict from seeing the letters how the word will be pronounced, or vice versa. English is particularly difficult in this respect, as we can see from groups of words like *bough, bow* (of a ship, or of a head) and *bow* (the weapon or the knot), where the second sounds like the first, but looks like the third. Many other languages show a much better correspondence between sounds and letters, such as Finnish or Spanish, and some of course, like Irish Gaelic, have a much worse relationship. But the general point should be clear: if we want to talk about speech-sounds accurately and unambiguously, we need to use an alphabet devised for this purpose, and this is one of the things which phonetics trains people to do.

Another reason for devising a special transcription is that we sometimes want to show differences between two people's pronunciation of the same word—when we are comparing dialects of a language, for example. If we want to write down how a Cockney speaker says the word *no*, as opposed to a Welshman, then it is no use taking the standard written form of the word, as all literate speakers of English spell it identically, regardless of how they pronounce it. We have to devise new, different 'spellings' to show the phonetic differences: thus we can indicate that the tongue moves from low in the front of the mouth to high in the back for the Cockney pronunciation by transcribing the word as [nau], and we can show that the tongue stays in one place, quite high up in the back of the mouth, for the Welsh pronunciation by transcribing it as [noː] (the colon here indicating that the vowel is relatively long in duration). Other differences could be shown in the same way. Sentences in phonetic transcription thus sometimes have an odd look about them; for example, one transcription of the sentence 'Jim's getting a rise next week' would be

$$[dʒɪmz gɛtɪŋ ə raɪz nɛks wiːk]$$

People are sometimes scared of phonetics because of this alien appearance. But if they remember why it is necessary to go to such lengths, and know what benefits can be obtained through using a phonetic transcription, then the strangeness should seem trivial, and the initial difficulty one is bound to have in mastering it should not be a deterrent.

Finally, I ought to reiterate the difference between the academic phonetician and the elocutionist, already mentioned on p. 8. The elocutionist endeavours to make a person's speech conform to a particular standard; the phonetician tries to describe the characteristics of everyone's speech as they are, and never has any intention of training people to adopt a different set of vocal manners for using their native language. The sounds are studied as ends in themselves, and not as the means to a further, aesthetic or social end. Phonetics is thus essentially a descriptive, empirical study. It is also a general one, that is, it is not restricted to studying the sounds of any one language, or group of languages; it studies the features of all human sounds, whichever language they happen to occur in. This branch of Linguistics is accordingly often referred to as General Phonetics.

But language is not merely randomly articulated human noise, which would be something like the beginnings of baby-babbling. It is patterned noise—sound with organization. Out of the total range of sounds a human being can produce, only a limited number are used in any one language. We refer to the kinds of sound which occur in a given language and the patterns into which they fall as the *sound system* of that language, and the study of sound systems is called *phonology*. Phonology is different from phonetics in that whereas phonetics studies sounds without restricting its attention to any one language, phonology deals with sounds only within the context of some specific language. It studies the *function* of sounds, which in the first instance is to identify words and word-groups and to distinguish words with different meanings. When we talk about 'the vowel system of English', 'the consonant sounds of German', or 'the intonation of Arabic', we are making phonological statements. When we talk about 'bilabial consonants in general', or 'the nature of melody, or pitch movement, in speech', without further qualification, our study is going to be a primarily phonetic one. The distinction between phonetics and phonology is theoretically very important, though of course we must remember that in analysing a real language, we are constantly carrying out both a phonetic and a phonological analysis, and moving from one point of view to the other.

We can illustrate this distinction very clearly by looking at some of the sounds which occur in English from both points of view. We shall take two sounds which are phonetically quite distinct, but which phonologically can be shown to be but two versions of a single basic entity. (Phonological entities are transscribed within slant lines, which show that what is being referred to is functioning as part of a specific linguistic system.) The /l/ sounds in the words *leap* and *peel* are pronounced very differently in most dialects of English. The first, sometimes called a 'clear' [l], is articulated with one part of the tongue (at the tip) touching the gum behind the top teeth, another part of the tongue being raised simultaneously to near the front portion of the roof of the mouth. If we say *leap* very slowly, spending a long time on the [l], this articulation can be clearly felt. (We can get an even clearer picture of where the tongue is by very sharply breathing in through the mouth while

keeping the tongue steady in this position: the cold air will
rush past the part of the tongue involved in the production
of the sound and give a very clear sensation of where in the
mouth it is.) The second kind of /l/, sometimes called a 'dark'
[ł], and distinguished by a slightly different symbol in transcription, is in a very different place, however: the tip of the
tongue stays behind the front teeth for the sound, but the part
which is raised towards the roof of the mouth is now much
further back—a good inch away. From the phonetic point of
view, therefore, there are two quite distinct sounds for /l/ in
English; and once we have learned to listen for the difference,
we can distinguish one from the other quite readily.

If we now consider these sounds from the phonological
viewpoint, we reach a different conclusion, the two sounds being
seen as fundamentally the same, having a single job to do. The
reason is that the language organizes these sounds so that they
have exactly the same function in helping to communicate and
distinguish between words and meanings, despite their differences
in pronunciation. The /l/ sounds, to begin with, do not occur
haphazardly: there is no question of our using clear [l] one
moment, and dark [ł] the next, depending on how we happen to
feel at the time. We are restricted in our use of the sounds; and
if we look carefully at the way in which they are distributed in
the words of the language, we find that the restrictions form a
nicely complementary pattern: we use clear [l] before a vowel,
and dark [ł] at the end of a word after a vowel, or before a
consonant. This is a very important discovery, because it accounts
for the central phonological fact about this pair of sounds, namely,
that we cannot make use of the contrast between them to help
build up words which are different in meaning—as we can with,
say, [p] and [t]. If we substitute a [p] sound for the [t] sound in the
word *cut*, we get a different word—which shows that [p] and [t]
are sounds which have an important role to play in distinguishing
meanings in English. But substitute a clear [l] for a dark [ł] in any
English word, and we do not get a different meaning: we get

D

the same word with a slightly odd accent. In this way we can show that the two kinds of /l/ are really one, from the point of view of the job they do in identifying meanings. The large phonetic difference is not matched by a corresponding phonological one. There is one phonological unit (or *phoneme*) only, which appears in two different forms, its sound depending on whereabouts in a word it happens to be.

This example also illustrates the statement that phonology is concerned with the study of the sound system of a particular language, and that the conclusions we reach about the phonology of one language should never be generalized into the study of another. Just because in English the /l/ situation is as above, we must not run away with the impression that these sounds function the same way in other languages, for we would soon be shown wrong. In Russian, for example, a similar phonetic difference to that between [l] and [ł] *does* carry with it a phonological difference: there are pairs of words, different in meaning, where the only phonetic difference is in the l-sounds used, for example, the words for *hatch* (of a ship) and *onion* are люк and лук respectively, the first beginning with a clear [l], the second with a dark kind.

There are many other examples of differences at the phonetic level which are unimportant at the phonological level. We have already mentioned the phonetic differences between the initial sounds of the words *keep* and *car* (p. 37), and these show a similar phonological relationship to that postulated for the English clear and dark /l/. Other examples would be the different /p/ sounds in words like *pin* and *spin*, where the first is pronounced with aspiration after the plosive, the second is not (the difference can be clearly felt if we hold the back of a hand up against our lips while saying them); or the /t/ sounds in words like *take* where there is aspiration, *stake* where there is none, and *outpost* where in most dialects there is no explosion for the plosive at all, due to the presence of the following [p] sound which 'covers' it.

A full statement of all such variations in sound in a language, so as to determine which variations cause differences in meaning and which do not, is clearly quite a complex matter; but it is a crucial thing to be able to do. Otherwise we have no way of imposing some order on the welter of sounds we use and hear used around us. We can easily underestimate the infinitude of insignificant minute differences which exist between our many pronunciations of different sounds. It can be shown without difficulty that the way I make a [t] sound, for example, differs from the way everyone else makes it, and, moreover, that it is highly unlikely that I could pronounce exactly the same [t] sound—exact in every phonetic detail—twice running. When one considers all the variables which I would have to keep constant, it should not be difficult to believe this: I should have to keep my tongue in an identical position behind the teeth, move it at the same speed away from the teeth, keep the pressure of air from my lungs absolutely stable, and so on. The slightest change in any of these factors would cause a difference in the quality of the sound, which it might be difficult or impossible to hear, but which techniques of acoustic analysis could clearly display. And if we consider the unlikelihood of two people having precisely the same dimensions for their vocal organs, and, in consequence, the unlikelihood of two absolutely identical articulations, then the surprising thing is that we can communicate with each other at all! But despite all these factors suggesting chaos, people do find themselves able to identify and discriminate sounds systematically in the vocal noise occurring around them —as long as they understand the language. Somehow a [t] sound remains a [t] sound, no matter who pronounces it, or where: we recognize it as a [t], and not as a [p] or a [k] or some other, and we automatically discount any phonetic minutiae which accompany it. Phonology is really no more than the study of the way in which language allows us to carry out this vastly complex task with unselfconscious ease.

The concept of phonology leads us on to the third aspect of language which we may distinguish. If phonology studies the

'organized noise' of language, we are entitled to ask: What is this
noise organized into? The answer is familiar: words, idioms,
phrases, clauses, sentences, and so on—what we would normally
refer to as the *grammar* and *vocabulary* of the language. We shall
discuss these two concepts in turn. Grammar is seen these days as
being the central part of Linguistics. (To some scholars, indeed,
grammar *is* Linguistics.) The task of the linguist in studying
the grammar of a language is to explain how we use sentences. A
grammar is really a way of putting down on paper what the
sentences of a language consist of, and how they relate to each
other. But this must be looked upon as a creative task. Grammar
should *not* be seen simply as a method of parsing clauses, though
this is unfortunately all that grammar does mean to many people.
Parsing is nothing more than a mechanical way of cutting up
sentences into bits and labelling them—a kind of linguistic post
mortem. Once we have labelled the bits, the job seems to be
over. No one ever explains why the job was carried out in the
first place (apart from vague talk about it being a 'discipline for
the mind'), and no one ever seems to want to put the sentences
back together again. But it is this last, constructive task which is
the only thing which will ever put grammar in touch with
reality. Linguists are trying to see grammar as a much more
'alive' feature of language than hitherto. They see it as the means
whereby human beings can communicate at all; as a dynamic
force which allows us to speak and understand hundreds of new
sentences every day—and after all most of the sentences we hear
we have never heard before. Grammar must be seen as a means
towards the end of explaining the complexities of a language's
structure. Once looked at in this more creative way, it becomes
more meaningful and of potential value. The linguists' shift
in attitude, then, is towards showing how sentences in language
are built up, rather than how they are broken down. This shift
can also be seen by emphasizing his opposition to thinking of
grammar as something contained in a book. This again is the
'corpse-based' approach. Grammar is so complex a thing that no

language has ever had the entirety of its grammar described. And we must also remember the factor of language change, which we have already had cause to discuss (p. 23): grammar books are always falling out of date. To place all our trust in a grammar book of any kind, and to subordinate our own intuitions about language to that of some past scholar, is really a very upside-down way of looking at things.

We can perhaps better appreciate the interest and magnitude of the grammarian's job if we look briefly at some of the problems he is faced with in trying to compose a grammar. His task, essentially, is to discover those rules in a language which are the basis of our being able to tell which sentences in that language are grammatical and acceptable, and which are not; he must show us what these sentences consist of, and how they relate to each other. Consequently his task falls into two parts: he must find out what the rules are; and he must devise some convenient and precise means of expressing them. Some rules are of course obvious, and do not cause any problems; for example, the rules which say that in English the article always precedes the noun, that the verb agrees with its subject in number, that the normal order for statements is subject before predicate, and so on. Other rules are not so obvious, however. It is not easy to discover the rules which govern the position of adverbs in a sentence, or say which verbs can take a passive, or predict the order in which a sequence of adjectives may occur.

Let us take this last point further. We may not have noticed that, in English, if we want to utter a sequence of adjectives before some noun, then we cannot do anything we like: there are a number of restrictions on which adjective may precede which. These restrictions do not apply to all adjectives (for example, we may say either 'it was a pleasant comfortable spot' or 'it was a comfortable pleasant spot'), but they affect a good number, as can be shown by the general unacceptability of such sentences as '*I can see a brown tall chimney' and '*There is a black big sheep'. (The asterisk is used to indicate that what follows is an ungrammatical utterance.) Scholars have tried to account for these restrictions by grouping adjectives into classes, calling them 'adjectives of age', 'adjectives of dimension', 'adjectives of colour', and so on, and then suggesting rules such as 'adjectives of dimension precede adjectives of colour', on the basis of the sentences they have observed. But there are many apparent exceptions to every rule (e.g. 'I have a pink big toe'), and no one has yet specified all the factors which contribute to one order of adjectives being more likely than another. It is a lack of knowledge of this kind which the grammarian seeks to remedy.

There are other problems involved in finding rules which will account for usage. Let us take the familiar relation of subject to predicate. Nouns as subject go before verbs in English; but it is not the case that *any* noun can precede *any* verb. There are important restrictions on their co-occurrence. For example, after observing such sentences as 'The boy is eating fish' and 'The horse sleeps in a stable', and noting that sentences such as '*The stone eats . . .' or '*The car sleeps . . .' do not occur, and are unacceptable, we would feel justified in subclassifying nouns and verbs into two types, calling them 'animate' and 'inanimate', let us say, and setting up a rule which says that 'animate nouns require animate verbs, and vice versa'. Such a rule is necessary if we hope to explain why restrictions of this type exist. But the task of formulating this rule precisely is not yet over, for while it satisfactorily explains the restrictions operating on a large number of sentences, it does not account for every single one. It does not explain why such sentences as 'My car eats up petrol' and 'This hotel sleeps thirty people' are acceptable. Clearly there is much more to the subject-predicate relationship than at first seems, and the grammarian has to establish what is happening here, suggest reasons for the apparent exceptions. He cannot hide behind this word 'exceptions', of course. To say that something is an 'exception' to a rule is not helpful, as it explains nothing. He has to go further than this, and define the rules which govern the use of the exceptions as well as those which govern the regular forms.

Another problem which faces the grammarian is how to distinguish between different senses of one sentence, or between different sentences which are superficially similar. For example, when faced with a sentence in isolation such as 'giant waves down funnel' (which one might well see as a newspaper headline), he must say more than simply 'this is ambiguous'. He must show where the ambiguity lies—that is, explain that 'giant' could be either adjective or singular noun, and 'waves' either plural noun or the third person singular of a verb. More complex and interesting cases can be found—the multiple ambiguity of 'The police were ordered to stop drinking after midnight', for example, where there are four distinct senses derivable from the same sequence of words. These are cases of one sentence with a number of possible interpretations. When more than one sentence is involved, then the grammarian has to beware taking them at their face value, and must not be misled into thinking that just because two sentences look the same on the surface that they have the same basic or underlying structure. If we compare such pairs of sentences as 'It was raining cats and dogs' and 'He was selling cats and dogs', 'I came across the road on a map' and 'I came across the road on a bicycle', 'I was kicked by a man' and 'I was kicked by a bus-stop', we can see that while there is an undeniable similarity, there are more fundamental differences, which we can readily sense, though perhaps find it difficult to explain. To take the first pair as a case in point, it is no answer to say that the first sentence is an 'idiom' whereas the second is not. We must go on to explain what we mean by 'idiom', and this means showing the differences in grammar between the two sentences as well as the differences in meaning. One technique of doing this is to show that we can manipulate the first sentence in ways that we cannot apply to the second, or vice versa: for example, we can turn the object of the second sentence into the singular ('He was selling a cat and a dog') but not the first ('*It was raining a cat and a dog'); we can add adjectives to the second ('He was selling nice cats and big dogs') but not to the first ('*It was raining nice cats and big dogs'), we can change the order of nouns in the second ('He was selling dogs and cats') but not in the first ('*It was raining dogs and cats'), and so on. In this way we can build up a picture of the extent of the grammatical difference between these two sentences, and we can work similarly for any other related utterances.

One of the grammarian's tasks is therefore to point out any significant differences which underlie similar looking structures. Another is to show underlying similarities between superficially different looking structures. For example, an active sentence in English looks very different from a passive one ('The man kicked the ball', 'The ball was kicked by the man'), but it is important to be told that they are related to each other in a very predictable way, and that one can be 'derived' from the other. Less obviously, interrogative sentences are related, not only to statements, but to relative clauses (compare 'Who saw you?' and 'The man who saw you is . . .'). In this way, a whole network of interrelationships between sentence-types can be established.

The grammarian must also notice and be able to handle sentences with a restricted usage, which only occur in a specialist, literary or humorous context. 'He danced his did' (E. E. Cummings) is acceptable in a literary context, but nowhere else; the word 'theirhisnothis' appears in Joyce's *Ulysses* as one word, not four; personification can disturb normal patterns of co-occurrence ('the sun smiled'); and so on. All such deviations from the rules of everyday speech have to be explained, if a grammar of a language is to be complete.

Finally, in this brief look at grammar, it is important to realize that the grammarian should express himself clearly and economically, and not make descriptive statements which are obscured behind a pile of verbiage. It is clearer, as well as more convenient, to say

$$S \longrightarrow Su\ P\ C\ (A)$$

than to say 'A sentence in English normally consists of a subject, predicator, complement and adverbial, the latter being optional', as long as one is familiar with the symbols used. Again, to express the relationship between active and passive verbally is quite cumbersome: 'The subject of the active sentence becomes the agent of the passive sentence, being placed after the verb, with the preposition "by" immediately before it; the object of the active sentence becomes the subject of the passive sentence; the verb is put into the past participial form and an auxiliary verb introduced'. This certainly explains the relationship between 'X kicked Y' and 'Y was kicked by X'; but it is much easier to write a rule as follows:

$$S + V + O \longrightarrow O + Aux + V_{pp} + by + S$$

In grammatical textbooks these days, one will see many rules cast in this or similar form. Ultimately such formulations are easier to write and understand than their longhand counterparts; and it is important that we should not let ourselves be put off by the mere sight of grammatical terminology and symbols, but make the effort to see what lies behind their use. If we do this, we find that our awareness of the structure of a language can be greatly increased.

The vocabulary, or lexicon, of a language, is also a familiar branch of study, in view of the fact that we are all used to handling dictionaries, in which the lexicon of a language is partially presented. So far, linguists have not studied in much detail the way the vocabulary of a language works, but clearly there are many issues which have got to be covered, for example, describing the various types of idioms which exist, demonstrating the ways in which words relate to each other and to a large extent define each other (such as with synonyms and antonyms), and showing how words tend to work in clusters to cut up aspects of the world in a particular way (the words for colours dividing up the colour spectrum, for instance, which differ from language to language). But at this point we have really ceased to talk

only about the forms of language, we have begun to talk about
their meanings also. The need to distinguish form from meaning
in language has already been emphasized when we were discussing parts of speech in traditional grammar (p. 21). Grammar
is essentially a formal study; we do not need to explain what
words mean to show how they group themselves into different
syntactic patterns. The meaning of words and sentences is not a
relevant part of their grammatical study: in grammar, we want
to say that 'boy' is a noun, that it occurs at such-and-such a place
in the sentence, that it has a plural 'boys', that it can be in the
genitive case, that it is a countable noun, and so on; we do not
want to say that 'boy' refers to 'a male child below the age of
puberty', which is what a dictionary might tell us. The study of
the meaning of linguistic forms is *semantics*, which is the final
aspect of language's structure which we have to consider.

Language is not simply patterns of noise. No matter how
systematic noise is, it cannot be language until it has been
given a meaning; and it derives this meaning largely from its
use in real-life situations. Language does not exist in a vacuum:
it has no independent existence apart from its users and the uses
to which we put it. We 'read' meanings into words and sentences
by seeing how they are used. A sequence of sounds remains
nonsense until we see how people are using it in relation to some
aspect of our experience. I might introduce a new word at this
moment, 'spled'; but until I have 'explained what I mean' by
the word, that is, shown what the word refers to in your and my
experience, it remains nonsense. If I now say that by 'spled' I
mean 'the number of letters in each line of print on each page', I
can go on to make such sentences as 'the spleds do not differ
a great deal', and be reasonably sure of being understood. What
I have done, in other words, is 'given' the word meaning, a
process which in a less arbitrary fashion is a standard part of our
normal use of language. Semantics thus studies the meaning or
meanings of linguistic forms. It does this firstly by showing how
these forms relate to each other (for example, one way of defining

a word like 'good' is to tell someone what its opposite is, another way is to give various equivalents—synonyms—and so on); and secondly, by looking at the relationship which exists between these forms and the phenomena the forms refer to in the 'outside world', what used to be referred to as the link between 'names' and 'things'—a very oversimplified and unsatisfactory way of putting it, but with a grain of truth in it none the less. The linguist is not concerned to study the nature of the 'things' themselves, of course; this is a job for others, such as the chemist, the philosopher, the geologist. What the linguist studies is the *relationship* which he sees to exist between language and things which are clearly not language. It is this which has gone on under the heading of the science of meaning, semantics. The field has been remarkably little investigated by linguists, and it is likely that significant developments in the study of meaning will be made in the very near future. Meanwhile, we must be aware of this aspect of language as being the province of a distinct branch of Linguistics, which can be studied independently of grammar, phonology and phonetics, but which works along with these to produce the total complex which we refer to as language.

The study of phonetics, phonology and grammar is the area which has occupied the linguist most over the past fifty years. Linguistic studies of vocabulary and semantics have hardly begun. But there is still a great deal to be discovered about even the more familiar aspects of language structure, and many scholars have begun to specialize in various corners of language in order to go more deeply into their complexity. Linguistics as a whole, in fact, is no longer a small, well-defined, homogeneous subject; it has begun to fragment, and these days it is possible to see a number of distinct emphases. There are at least five important 'strands' to the subject. Three of these we have already mentioned in our earlier discussion. First there is the study of certain fundamental topics connected with the nature of language, such as the relation between speech and writing, or between historical and non-historical study, which really provides an elementary grounding in linguistic ideas. Second, there is the descriptive strand, the aim here being to make a full description of some aspect of a language group, language, dialect or idiolect (that part of the overall language system made use of by one individual); and, closely related to this, the comparative side of Linguistics, which aims to show the similarities and differences between various languages, dialects, etc. Thirdly, we have seen that Linguistics has a very practical side, which is intended to equip people for the descriptive work just referred to. There are established techniques for finding out how a language works, just as there are for finding out how anything works—techniques which will produce an ability to hear the sounds of a language accurately, to be able to describe them, and write them down, using a phonetic transcription; techniques for finding out what the smallest units of grammar are; techniques for assessing the way in which the speakers of a language provide one with information; and so on. These would all be part of the first two years of any linguist's training.

There is also a very important theoretical side to Linguistics, and this happens to be particularly controversial at the present time. Linguists ultimately want to be able to establish a theory about how language works which will define and interrelate all the concepts that we feel are essential to describe a language adequately—concepts like 'consonant', 'syllable', 'noun', 'tense', 'mood', 'word' and 'sentence'. It is not easy to define such labels; the sentence alone has had well over a hundred definitions; and we have already seen the danger inherent in the traditional approach to the definition of the parts of speech. Devising a linguistic theory is not a simple matter, and there are currently a number of different theories about language being worked out. People who begin to study Linguistics in depth will soon come across labels like 'generative', 'scale-and-category' and 'stratificational', adjectives which refer to different kinds of grammatical theory, and they will hear frequent mention of

'Chomskyan' or 'Neo-Firthian' schools of linguistic thinking. These are merely labels which have been attached to different approaches to the study of language, the proper names usually stemming from the names of the scholars who devised them. There are always certain similarities between the different theories, of course, but these are usually far outweighed by the differences. There are, consequently, many controversial issues, and sometimes the arguments involved are obscure, and difficult to understand even for those who are specialists in linguistic theory. Some aspects of linguistic theory are also couched in very mathematical or logical terms, with a superficially fearsome symbology, and this can put people off unless they are prepared for it. A further difficulty in studying this field is the tendency for a theory to fragment once it has begun to be expounded. A theory, one must remember, is the brainchild of an individual, who develops it over the years, and simultaneously teaches it to his students; these students then develop their own versions of the original theory, many variants arise, and further controversy is the result. The kind of grammar known as 'generative grammar' only became widely known in 1957, but nowadays there are many kinds of generative grammar, not all of which are mutually compatible. A student needs careful supervision here, and should leave this part of Linguistics to a more advanced stage of study.

Finally, there is an 'applied' strand to Linguistics—the study of language not as an end in itself, but as the means to the furtherance of some other, non-linguistic end, such as the teaching of modern languages. I shall be discussing this side of the subject separately in Chapter 3, so I shall not go into it here, but simply say that the more one studies Linguistics, the more fields one comes across where its findings could be of value.

To survey these different strands of Linguistics is of course to highlight some of the difficulties in the way of anyone who wants to study the subject seriously. One has to re-think many basic, and possibly long-established ideas. If one has been happily teaching English through Latin, for example, then to study Linguistics means that one must be prepared to adopt a very different method and scale of values, and this can be very difficult. Also, there is the absence of a generally-agreed theoretical basis for the whole of the subject, and this could disturb someone who likes a field of study to be founded on well-established general principles. Personally, I find the lack of general theoretical agreement, the fact of controversy, not so much disturbing as exciting. Moreover, this situation is hardly peculiar to Linguistics: all sciences have to go through a period of theoretical adolescence; and Linguistics, one must remember, is very much an adolescent as scientific disciplines go. But even those in the well-established sciences seem to like re-examining the bases of their knowledge quite regularly—the present concern to determine the theoretical foundations of physics being a case in point.

Yet another feature of Linguistics which often disturbs enquirers is the unfamiliar terminology which linguists have devised to talk precisely about language—terms like 'phoneme', 'morpheme', 'nominal group', 'bilabial fricative', 'collocation', and so on. These are often criticized as 'jargon'. In fact, jargon—if all one means by this is 'technical terms'—is an essential part of the apparatus of any intellectual discipline; and the terminology of Linguistics is no more technical than that of many other modern sciences, and certainly no more technical than the terminology used in traditional grammar (which was in any case extremely imprecise). Critics of linguistic terminology often seem to imply that one does not need to be precise in order to talk about language, that just because language is a more familiar world than, say, chemistry or electron physics, one can talk about it using familiar terms. Nothing could be further from the truth, as our experience of traditional language study has shown. In fact the total number of important technical terms that Linguistics makes regular use of is extremely small—some three or four dozen. Some of the advanced theories do make use of a whole battery of exotic terms, and are expressed in weird symbols; but no one would begin their studies with such theories, consequently the existence of such terms cannot be adduced as a reason for putting beginners off.

To study Linguistics, in short, one has to be a bit of a schizophrenic. One has to have two kinds of mind: the analytic, jig-saw puzzle mind, on the one hand, which will enable one to enjoy looking at a mass of language data and trying to discern patterns there; and the speculative, imaginative mind, which allows one to think about some of the more philosophical and theoretical issues in language. The 'compleat linguist' should have some knowledge of practical phonetics as well as of the nature of meaning. Of the two sides, the practical and theoretical, the former is probably the more basic. One can do a lot of useful descriptive work without embarking on flights of linguistic fancy, without having speculated very much about points of theory; but useful theoretical work cannot be done well unless one has had a solid grounding in practical analysis.

In referring to the analytic mind, above, I used the word 'enjoy'. This is important. Unless an individual has a fairly strong interest in languages, and feels a definite impulse to study them in greater depth, then he is strongly advised to keep away from Linguistics, as the inculcating of the basic analytic skills, and the meticulous examination of language data can, without this initial interest, drive him near to desperation. With most university subjects, a sixth former can be reasonably sure that he knows the kind of thing which will be studied once he is at university, as he has probably studied the subject already in his school career. But with academic subjects like Philosophy and Linguistics, which are not taught in schools, he can have much less of an idea of what is involved—unless he is lucky enough, as was mentioned earlier, to have a knowledgeable careers master, or has enough initiative to read up something about the subject first. Linguistics is much worse off than Philosophy, too, in view of its recent development.

Anyone who is thinking of taking up Linguistics is therefore strongly advised to meditate very carefully about what the subject involves. I know of many prospective university students who have been interviewed to read for a degree in Linguistics, but who have not really thought about the subject at all, and who, one suspects, are really only looking for something new, perhaps something not associated with the routine of school life. These applicants may have a vague interest in languages, and they usually admit to a liking for learning languages—but this is hardly enough. It would seem positively foolish to apply for a university course on this basis, to commit oneself to four years of study of a subject one knows nothing about, particularly if one does not have the kind of mind appropriate for such study. Just because Linguistics is in the Arts Faculty of most universities, and linked with departments of Modern Languages, Classics and English, one forgets that the subject is in many respects a science, and has a great deal in common with the Science Faculty also. (The department at Reading University, for example, is officially called Linguistic Science, though it is none the less in the Faculty of Letters.) Linguistics is one of those subjects which overlaps the two cultures. For many people, indeed, it is precisely this which is the basis of its appeal.

CHAPTER THREE

The Uses of Linguistics

Even after one explains to people in general terms what Linguistics is about, there remains a question which recurs with great frequency, namely, Why study language in this way at all? Or simply, Why study language? There are a number of ways to tackle such a question. One can simply take a leaf out of the mountaineer's book and say 'I study language because it's there', 'because it's interesting', and so on, which is perhaps the best reason of all. Or one can point to the widespread ignorance which exists at both popular and scholarly levels about the nature of language, and argue that this should be remedied. Or one can turn the question round and ask, Why study sixteenth-century literature, or ancient history? and argue that studying language as an end in itself is no less useful. But what enquirers are usually most interested in is understanding the linguist's role in relation to the practical value of Linguistics for different corners of society. And as soon as one starts to follow this line of argument, one finds that there are a number of related questions which interest people, particularly if they are thinking of their careers, such as, What can somebody *do* with Linguistics once he has studied it, whether to degree level or any other? What sort of jobs are there for people trained in this way? These are difficult questions to be final about, for so far relatively few people have been trained exclusively in the subject. But one can see that there are, broadly speaking, three kinds of answer that might be given.

First of all, a qualification in Linguistics can be viewed as a qualification, and no more—a statement of a standard reached in

an intellectual discipline, and thus on a par with other qualifications at the same level. A B.A. in Linguistics, from this point
of view, has precisely the same value as a B.A. in any other
subject. And for many occupations in social, industrial or public
life, this is the crucial point: one must have a degree, or a
diploma, or something, and the higher the grade attained the
better. Exactly what kind of subject the qualification is in is not
important, as the student will probably be trained from scratch
in his new job anyway. All an arts degree, for example, guarantees
an employer in one of these fields is a certain amount of ability
on the part of a student; it guarantees that the student has pursued
the study of some subject in depth, used his initiative in study,
and so on. In this sense, therefore, Linguistics has the same status
and general value as any other academic subject which one might
read. One is not particularly concerned with making further use
of the subject once the university has been left behind.

However, what can a person do with Linguistics if he *does*
want to follow it up in some way, and make use of the information he has had about language in the course of his professional
career? Again, Linguistics is no different from many other
subjects, in that there are two possible answers to this question,
depending on whether the 'pure' or the 'applied' side of the
subject is being emphasized. As far as 'pure' interest in Linguistics
is concerned, it is of course possible, after initial training, to do
research into Linguistics. As we have seen from Chapter 2, there
is plenty of this still to be done. One way of using one's linguistic
skills, then, would be to do postgraduate research in some
university, or find a post which would allow time for research,
or where it was a condition of appointment that research of some
kind was done. Jobs in universities and other places of higher
education, both in Great Britain and abroad, would fall into
this category; and there are quite a number of research projects
into various aspects of language sponsored by the governments
of different countries or by major industrial bodies—on
machine translation, or the development of reading skills in

children, for example. There are also many non-linguistic projects in higher education where a trained linguist is a much-needed and highly valued member of a research team—work in computers, sociology, psychology and education in particular. This, then, is one side of the situation, as far as 'using' Linguistics is concerned. As one might expect, with specialist work of this type, jobs are relatively few, and qualifications required for appointment are high. It is in the many facets of *applied linguistics* that the real opportunities to make use of one's linguistic talents are to be found, and we shall spend the remainder of this chapter discussing some of the more important areas covered by this label.

By 'applied linguistics' I mean the application of linguistic methodology, techniques of analysis and research findings to some non-linguistic field. Linguistics in this sense is thus very much a means to some end, rather than an end in itself. There are many such fields, and there is still much work to be done. The first, and major application of linguistic research is of course in the field of language teaching and language learning—especially in the teaching of *foreign* languages. The term 'applied linguistics' has even at times been used as if it were synonymous with 'foreign language teaching'. The relevance of Linguistics in this field should be fairly obvious. It should be a truism that one cannot teach a language without first of all knowing about it, but unfortunately it is not. The operative word in this sentence is, of course, 'about'. To 'know about' a language is not the same thing as to 'know' a language. Being able to speak a language fluently is no guarantee that one is able to explain and present it to others to learn (cf. p. 7). Amateurism here is dangerous. One comes across so many cases of people who have been taught the wrong facts about a language, because the teacher has not been properly trained, or who have given up learning a language in despair because the information they were being given had not been graded properly. Proper training in this context means a great deal. It means being aware of the facts of a language as displayed and interrelated within the framework of some theory; it means being up to date in awareness of research into the nature of any of these facts; it means being able to select and grade these facts within the restrictions of a specific course; it means being able to criticise constructively the available teaching handbooks; it means bearing in mind the differences between the language the learner already knows and the one he is trying to learn, so that points of difficulty can be more readily anticipated and prepared for; and there is much more.

Institutions are becoming increasingly aware of the need for adequately trained teachers of language, especially of the spoken language; and there are now many openings for linguistically orientated teachers both in Great Britain and abroad. Teaching English as a foreign language is the major industry in this field. Organizations like the British Council perform an invaluable role in providing for the training in Linguistics of many teachers of English overseas. Diplomas in Applied Linguistics or in English as a Foreign Language antedate undergraduate courses in Linguistics in this country by many years, and are much more widespread. This interest is not very surprising. English is a major language of international communication; it is the official language of education and government in many countries; it is certainly the most widely learned second language. And there is an incessant demand from all over the world for competent teachers of English at all levels, in primary schools and upwards. Moreover, this demand is equalled, if not exceeded, by the call for textbooks which are linguistically enlightened. There are hundreds of courses on the English language, but few of these take account of the findings of linguists about English which have taken place over the last twenty or so years; and what I am saying about English could be repeated to a lesser degree about every other major European language.

Linguistics is also percolating very slowly into schools in this country and the United States, in connection with the teaching of foreign languages to English-speaking people. A qualification in Linguistics is now no longer looked upon with suspicion by most headmasters. It is more usually seen as a way of improving the quality of language teaching. This is not before time. We are all familiar with the situation of the schoolboy who uses 'school French' on his first visit to France, and finds he is unable to understand or make himself understood! People are now beginning to realize that this situation is a symptom of a fundamental disorder in foreign language teaching. It is not too much to hope that Linguistics may be able to help a little here. In particular one could point to the vast need for teachers of the more 'exotic' languages like Russian or Chinese in our schools and in higher education. Intensive training in such languages is much facilitated if carried on within a perspective of General Linguistics. The increasing use of language laboratories in schools is another step along the right lines—but here one must beware of thinking that one has found the answer simply by possessing a lot of expensive equipment. A language laboratory is no replacement for a thorough training in linguistic principles. A language laboratory is, after all, only as good as the material on the tapes being used. If the tapes are bad, no amount of mechanical ingenuity will improve the standard of a pupil's fluency. But to get good tapes, one needs to be fully aware of the complexities of language and the problems involved in grading structures on the basis of linguistic and pedagogical criteria. Again a linguistic orientation is essential.

Linguistics has not yet made much headway in the other main aspect of language teaching, the teaching of an individual's first, or 'native' language. In Great Britain, for example, despite a great deal of criticism of existing English Language examinations, and the recommendations of various bodies (cf. p. 24), very little progress has actually been made in introducing Linguistics or linguistic ideas into the range of language subjects taught in schools. It is left to a teacher's own initiative. (The recently introduced sixth-form Use of English examination, let it be said once and for all, has nothing to do with Linguistics.) Exactly

how Linguistics might be systematically introduced into schools
is a question which has not really been probed as yet, although
organizations like the National Association for the Teaching of
English have begun to discuss it. There are two complementary
lines one might take. One might introduce Linguistics as such,
as an extra component of the curriculum, perhaps under some
such heading as 'general' or 'liberal' studies. In such a case, of
course, there would be no intention of improving anyone's
command of English or any other language; it would simply be
an attempt to instil into a student a conscious awareness of the
structure and potential of language in general, and of his own
language in particular. This may incidentally produce greater
efficiency in the student's use of a particular language, but the
'remedial' effect of the course would not be its primary aim.

Secondly, one might not introduce Linguistics as a special
subject at all, but bring it in as the basis of a course on a particular
language. Again, this would be essentially an informative course
on the nature of the language in question, not primarily designed
to improve anyone's command of it—though one can hardly
doubt that this would be one of the by-products. Moreover, it
could have a value as a mental discipline, the kind of value that
is often claimed for the study of Latin. One could also always
introduce a remedial component into such a course, if this was
required. There are many aspects of language, usually ignored in
courses on specific languages, which could be introduced with
relatively rapid therapeutic results—information about the
different styles of spoken and written language, for example, so
that the student becomes more conversant with the kinds of
language appropriate for such diverse situations as conversation,
formal discussion, letter-writing, and so on. And there are other
possibilities for Linguistics in the schools—for example, in the
teaching of reading and oral fluency in primary schools and
elsewhere. Many such fields are currently being investigated as
research projects, but little of this work is sufficiently advanced
to achieve any kind of general recognition.

Many people are agreed on the need for courses of some kind to fill the present gap in linguistic knowledge. The universities are now almost completely convinced about this, and at sixth-form conferences, and the like, the pupils themselves seem strongly attracted to the idea. In the United States experimental syllabuses for Linguistics in schools have also been successful. But there is no chance of introducing new courses into schools until teachers are ready to teach them, and this takes time. Many training-colleges now run courses in Linguistics, and we can expect a new climate of opinion to emerge before too long. But we still lack course-books and basic introductions; and until these have been written, Linguistics will not become a definite part of a school curriculum.

Apart from the different aspects of language-teaching, there are many other fields of applied linguistics that one could point to, but to do justice to them all would take a much larger book than this. Translation is a fairly obvious example, especially the developing field of translation through machines. One cannot programme a machine to do the translator's job unless one has given it a great deal of information. The machine needs to be told everything about the structure of the two languages it is supposed to be relating, *and* told how to go about finding the equivalences which we know exist; and most of this background only the linguist can provide. Another 'mechanical' field with work for the linguist is telecommunications in its many forms. Phonetics is extremely important in the field of telephone transmission, for instance. It costs money to send voices along wires, and if one can cut down on the amount of voice which needs to be transmitted, then clearly there would be a very great saving. The linguistic problem is therefore to determine which features of speech are essential for intelligibility and acceptability and which are not. Many of the non-essential features can then be disregarded as far as transmission is concerned. But to determine precisely which these features are involves research on a large scale, and this work still goes on.

One can imagine many other applications of linguistic information to mechanical techniques, some of which have hardly begun to be followed up. For example, it has been suggested that a new kind of 'visual deaf-aid' could be produced, using information obtained from acoustic phonetics. There is already in existence a machine which can produce a picture of speech sounds, though this picture is very complex, and difficult to read. The machine is called a sound spectrograph. Now if the pictures of the different sounds could be produced as a series of easily recognizable, schematized shapes, then one would in effect be turning speech directly into a kind of writing. One can even imagine a portable machine with an attached microphone and screen: one speaks into the microphone and the picture of what one says comes onto the screen. A deaf person, once he had learned this new 'alphabet', would then be able to 'read' the speech directly. A great deal of research would be needed to make such a device a commercial proposition, of course, and very little work has so far been carried out on it; but in principle one can see its potential value.

Of course we must not let our imaginations carry us too far away in thinking of mechanical applications of linguistic research. The science fiction world where men speak to robots and they answer back is unlikely to materialize for quite some time: we simply do not know enough about how to synthesize speech to make this a reality at the moment—let alone the technical problems of making the machines sufficiently small to be manageable. Even reading one's instructions out loud into a computer is a vast task which has still to be successfully completed; and here we are not expecting the computer to reply in the same terms!

We must also guard against premature application of linguistic ideas. It is not difficult to impress people with a linguistic point, in view of the fact that few people are capable of assessing it at all, and one must in principle be critical of what people claim they can do in the name of Linguistics, to avoid being led astray by an eccentric viewpoint which does not reflect general thinking in the field. For example, it has been claimed that the pictures of speech produced by the sound spectrograph contain information which will allow us, if trained, to identify the speaker (voice quality information basically, cf. p. 32–3); it is claimed that it is possible to pick out from ten sentences spoken by five people which sentences were produced by the same people. Now in principle there is no reason why this should not be the case, but there is very little experimental evidence available to show how it is to be done, and there is clear evidence to show that the method is not infallible. But recently a court in the United States accepted evidence based on information derived from these pictures of speech, or 'voiceprints', as they are called (presumably on the analogy of fingerprints). In this particular instance, therefore, application seems to be going ahead of theory.

Moving on now to a completely different area of applied linguistics, a rapidly developing relationship exists between Linguistics and the field of speech pathology. There are many kinds of language disorder, involving both the way in which we produce speech and the way in which we receive and comprehend it. Before any kind of therapy, however, there must be a clear picture of exactly what the linguistic deficiency is, and how far removed it is from normality. Is it a disorder of a phonetic, phonological, grammatical or semantic nature, or some combination of these? And if grammatical, then which aspect of grammar is being affected, and how deeply? To answer such questions, one obviously has to do two things: describe the speech habits of the patient, and relate these to a standard or scale of normal speech behaviour. This is easier said than done. In fact no linguistic standards of normality exist, on paper. Specialists rely on their experience, which of course varies; therapists tend to treat the most noticeable deviations in a person's speech, and are in danger of ignoring what could be more fundamental (albeit less obvious) aberrations; and no one is really clear as to what the speech-patterns of, say, a four-year-old child are. It is just such a lack of knowledge which the linguist is competent to remedy. He does not attempt to do the therapist's job; he simply tries to put at her disposal (it is usually a 'she') precise information about the linguistic state she is trying to help her patient to achieve.

So far we have been looking at fields marginal to Linguistics— fields which a linguist might turn his attention to, once trained, and which would not normally be part of his basic training. There are, however, other, so-called 'marginal' fields of study which remain to be discussed, fields which were once thought of as further areas in which Linguistics might profitably be applied, but which are these days increasingly thought of as an obligatory part of a linguist's training, and thus hardly qualify as 'applied' linguistics in any useful sense. Such fringe areas usually coincide with fairly obvious overlaps between different areas of academic study; thus one hears of philosophical linguistics, mathematical linguistics, computational linguistics, psycho- linguistics (psychology + linguistics) and sociolinguistics (socio- logy + linguistics). We have not really had cause to refer to many of the issues dealt with by these branches of the subject in this book, though over the last few pages we have referred to appli- cations of language study which would involve specialist training in one or other of them, for example, automatic translation and computational linguistics, speech pathology and psycholinguistics (note that there may be disorders of one's comprehension of speech as well as in one's articulation). I shall discuss one of the facets of sociolinguistics a little further, however, as it is a matter which has been raised a few times in earlier pages; this is usually labelled *stylistics*.

Stylistics in its most general sense refers to the application of linguistic techniques to the study of particular kinds of language current within a given speech community, such as the language of science, of law, of religion, of debate, or of literature, or the language of different social classes. It does not take much thought to realize that the language we make use of in everyday life varies a great deal, and that this variation depends on the kind of social situation we happen to be in. To take a simple case, the language we may use in talking to a baby is far removed from the language we would use in all other situations; we would never mistake it for anything else. And similarly, there are many different 'varieties' or 'styles' of language that we use in the appropriate situations. Stylistics studies which variety of speech or writing is appropriate to which situation, and tries to develop our awareness and control of these variations. We are taught some of these social differences from an early age, of course: 'Don't use such language to the vicar!' is an instruction to conform to one set of speech-habits appropriate in this situation and to avoid others. We learn a host of such restrictions from our earliest years. In school, we get a little more information about different varieties—when we are taught how to write a letter, for example, or an essay. But we are rarely given information about some of the really important conventions which exist around us and which we regularly come into contact with— the language habits of the law, the civil service, the advertisers, the scientists, and so forth. Very often we are unable to understand other people's ways of putting even non-technical matters across, or are fooled into accepting someone's point of view because of the way in which he argues it, or drop a linguistic brick, by using a 'non-U' word or phrase in a certain situation. In all such cases, it can be argued, we are simply showing a marked ignorance of how our own language works. Stylistics tries to remedy such situations, by showing us what is going on in a particular use of language. Once we know this, we tend to be in a much more confident frame of mind.

Consider an argument over a matter of interpretation, to illustrate this point. Person A thinks that the meaning of a piece of language (it may be a legal document, an income tax form, or a poem, for example) is one thing; person B thinks that it is another. To resolve the argument, their only chance is to carry out some kind of analysis of what the text actually says; and clearly the more systematic this is the better. In literary criticism, too, we require something a little more than our sensitive response to a poem or novel if we hope to get the most out of it. Our subjective impression of a poem is perfectly all right until some-one else comes along who disagrees with it. Then it is no good reiterating such phrases as 'But I like the poem', 'I think it's good'. This gets us nowhere, for the person who thinks the poem is bad will want reasons for our opinion. Again, the only thing is to try to rationalize the subjectivity inherent in our approach by looking at the language, and seeing what is in it which has caused such a favourable or unfavourable reaction. And as soon as we try to do this, we need ways and means of describing what is there. We are back with our linguistic techniques again. Stylistics can thus be of value to a number of people, including the sociologist, educationalist, psychologist, philosopher, literary critic, and man in the street, all of whom are interested in the use of language in society in one form or another.

I could go on to discuss many other tasks which the linguist could assist in, but I have probably given enough detailed illustration of the kind of use Linguistics has. Interesting research areas not already mentioned would include reading and spelling reform (consider the linguistic considerations which enter into any attempt to evaluate the Initial Teaching Alphabet, for example), questions of uncertain authorship (*did* St Paul write those Epistles, or Bacon those plays? can we obtain any evidence from the style?), and the desirability or otherwise of universal auxiliary languages (like Esperanto). We must also remember that any Linguistics course worth its salt will ensure that the student will have studied at least one language other than English in depth, and will be proficient in that language—it may be a European language, or something further afield. This means that the specialist careers involving competence in a particular foreign language or languages are open to the general linguist as much as to the man who did the whole of his degree in a language. The main difference between a degree in French, let us say, and one in French and Linguistics, or in Linguistics specializing in French, is the large amount of literature covered by the former; the extent to which the French language is studied is *at least* the same, and probably more fully comprehended in the case of the latter two because of the nature of the basic training.

Thus, apart from the fields already discussed, one could make a very long list of possible careers for the man trained in Linguistics who has specialized in modern languages. He could consider the following fields, all of which require language specialists of some kind: most of the branches of the Civil Service (especially the Diplomatic Service); the British Council, and other bodies concerned with international relations and exchange; public relations in general; the tourist industry; nationalized industries; public administration (especially in education); international organizations (such as U.N.E.S.C.O.); civil aviation; port authorities; commerce, banking and insurance; export industries and overseas companies; advertising; mass media concerns (broadcasting and journalism in particular—especially with their reliance on the 'foreign correspondent'); engineering; the hotel and catering industry; the armed forces; telephone and telegraph organizations; professional translating and interpreting (for example, in business, literary, governmental or scientific contexts); and, at a more domestic level, there are travel agencies, libraries, large department stores, and, of course, all kinds of secretarial work. There are jobs in all these fields for people with a good knowledge of one or more modern foreign languages, who have an ability to learn foreign languages, and —most important of all—who are not frightened by them.

Any field which is at all concerned with language can benefit from Linguistics. And, in the nature of things, it is difficult to think of an aspect of human behaviour which is not. The problem of self-expression and comprehension is a daily and universal one This, perhaps, is the main reason why we need to study language in any systematic way. Language is the most powerful means of communication we have—but only if it is used well. If used badly, it can be just as much a barrier to communication. The familiar phrase, 'they just don't seem to speak the same language' is levelled at people who fall out at all levels of society, whether they be husband and wife, employer and employee, opposing sides in government, or even opposing governments. We have all heard of strikes being caused by one side in a dispute taking hold of the wrong end of a verbal stick, or of business letters designed to appeal which have in fact repelled. Our language is probably the most sensitive side of us. And we have only to think of such words as 'democratic', to realize that two countries can use the same word but mean widely different things. The Iron Curtain, it has been wisely said, is also a semantic curtain.

Language is so essential to our everyday existence that we tend to take it for granted. Even when it is the cause of trouble, we tend to search for other reasons. But if we stop taking its existence for granted, and try to understand its complexity and the problems involved in its use, then perhaps a great deal of tears, toil and sweat will be avoided. Linguistic self-awareness is an ideal that is well worth trying for. And it is this which, to my mind, is the ultimate pragmatic justification for the subject introduced in this book.

For Further Reading

BASIC BACKGROUND READING. All the books in this section provide useful coverage of most fundamental linguistic issues; they are all relatively cheap, and, in my opinion, easy to read.

D. Abercrombie, *Problems and principles in language study* (Longman, 1956). A very useful and clear account of many of the fundamental theoretical and practical problems of language analysis, with a strong emphasis on English language teaching to foreigners, and on phonetic problems; there is also an interesting chapter on gesture.

R. A. Hall, *Linguistics and your Language* (Doubleday, 1960). A paperback introduction to the different components of General Linguistics, but paying special attention to popular and traditional notions about language. There is a clear exposition of much linguistic terminology.

O. Jespersen, *Mankind, nation and individual* (Allen & Unwin, 1946). This is a collection of essays on various basic questions to do with languages, such as the relationship between dialect and language, standards of correctness, and slang. It is a stimulating, personal viewpoint, putting many popular notions in a linguistic perspective, but is not an introduction to Linguistics as such.

E. Sapir, *Language* (Hart-Davis, Harvest Books, 1955). A paperback edition of a book written in 1921, one of the first systematic surveys of the phenomenon of language. It is a very personal view of the subject, reflecting Sapir's own interests, and it gives a clear and stimulating picture of both the general and practical sides of language study, accompanied by a wealth of comparative information. In view of its date, there is of course no coverage of the many theoretical and technical advances which have since taken place, but this does not reduce its value as essential introductory reading.

SOME GENERAL INTRODUCTIONS. All the books in this section provide a good coverage of linguistic principles and methods, and could be used as the basis for a thorough introductory course of study.

D. L. Bolinger, *Aspects of language* (Harcourt, Brace & World, 1968). A very lucid general account of the central topics involved in a linguistic approach to language study, with some excellent exemplification.

R. A. Hall, *Introductory linguistics* (Chilton Books, 1964). A very large and systematic review of the different components of linguistic study, designed as a course-book. Extremely easy to read, although at times rather selective. The emphasis is on the Romance languages, and there is useful bibliographical information.

J. Lyons, *Introduction to theoretical linguistics* (C.U.P., 1968). Thorough coverage of major contemporary theoretical problems, especially in syntax and semantics. Some sections deal with quite advanced issues. A fine initial account for serious students.

R. H. Robins, *General linguistics, an introductory survey* (Longman, 2nd edn., 1971). This provides a thorough coverage of all aspects of Linguistics, in slightly greater depth than the above. A very useful, but difficult, standard textbook, which takes a great deal for granted and should not be first reading in the subject without supervision.

D. A. Wilkins, *Linguistics in language teaching* (Arnold, 1972). A wide-ranging critical discussion of the extent to which linguistics is of value in the field of foreign-language teaching; aimed primarily at those professionally engaged in language teaching, but a useful perspective for anyone interested in the subject's applications.

The Pelican Linguistics series provides extensive introductory coverage of a number of branches of Linguistics. So far available are: D. Crystal, *Lingusitics* (1971), F. R. Palmer, *Grammar* (1971),

J. O'Connor, *Phonetics* (1973), G. Turner, *Stylistics* (1973), S. P. Corder, *Introducing Applied Linguistics* (1973).

BOOKS SPECIFICALLY ON ENGLISH. All the books in this section take one or more aspects of English and study these in depth within a linguistic framework of some kind. They should be read as much for the light they throw on linguistic principles and procedures as for their information about the English language as such.

D. Crystal & D. Davy, *Investigating English style* (Longman, 1969). An introductory examination of the different varieties of English speech and writing using the techniques of stylistics.

H. A. Gleason, Jr., *Linguistics and English grammar* (Holt, Rinehart & Winston, 1965). A survey of many different approaches to the study of English grammar, with a discussion of some central grammatical problems. Easy to read, with a useful survey of the history of Linguistics in the first few chapters.

F. R. Palmer, *The English verb* (Longman, 1965). A good illustration of the kind of detailed, systematic study which is produced by a specialist examination of one area of English grammar.

R. Quirk, *The use of English* (Longman, 2nd edn. 1968). An excellent, easy to read introduction to a wide variety of questions about the English language, with many fundamental linguistic issues discussed. Follow-up exercises are provided for further thinking; and the book also contains two very useful supplements, one by A. C. Gimson on the pronunciation of English, the other by J. Warburg on popular notions of correctness.

A. C. Gimson, *Introduction to the Pronunciation of English* (Arnold, 2nd edn., 1970). A clear, introductory presentation of methods of phonetic description, with details of the present-day English sound system.

BOOKS ON RELATED ISSUES

C. Cherry, *On human communication* (M. I. T. Press, 1957). Available in paperback, this provides an introduction to the notion of

F

communication from a number of different points of view, including linguistics, mathematics, psychology and cybernetics. A useful background book, though very selective on Linguistics.

E. T. Hall, *The silent language* (Fawcett Publications, 1959). A highly stimulating and influential paperback on non-vocal aspects of human behaviour which communicate information about ourselves and our culture.

Some Undergraduate Courses in Linguistics in British Universities

In order to give an idea of the kind of thing one would be committed to if one did an undergraduate degree course in Linguistics (with or without some other subject) in a British University, I have brought together details of courses taken from the Calendars of some of the universities which offer this subject for a main degree, at the time of writing. This information is of course intended only as an illustration of the way Linguistics tends to be formalized as an academic subject, and is in no sense an evaluation of the different courses, or an attempt to be a complete guide to the way the subject is taught in British universities. No reference is made to those places which allow the study of Linguistics as a special or subsidiary subject ancillary to one's main course, nor to postgraduate diplomas and degrees, which are well established in a number of places. A convenient source of information about many of the postgraduate courses covering Linguistics and English-language teaching is the British Council publication, *Academic Courses in Great Britain relevant for the Teaching of English as a Second Language*, which appears annually. One should also remember that Linguistics may be being taught in a university, not under its own name, but as a component of some other department's course, such as English or Modern Languages. It is also the case that new degree courses in Linguistics are coming into existence at more and more places, and up-to-date information about these can only really be obtained by writing to the registrar of any university doing this.

As a point of principle, *all* information in this section should be checked before making use of it, as universities tend to revise their syllabuses from time to time, and as there is no precedent for degree courses in Linguistics in this country, this might well happen quite often in the near future, until the most efficient kinds of course can be devised.

1. *University of Reading* (details from the Calendar, 1972–3, pp. 369ff., with 1974 alterations incorporated; a departmental brochure is available).

After an introductory two terms involving courses in 'General Characteristics of Language' and 'Basic Descriptive Techniques', students may choose one of the Honours courses as follows:
Linguistics as a Single Subject course. This extends over ten terms, including a whole year abroad. The Final Examination consists of papers in: 1. Phonetics and phonology. 2. Linguistic theory and the history of linguistics. 3, 4. *Two* of the following options: (*a*) Sociolinguistics and dialectology, (*b*) Second language learning, (*c*) Child language acquisition, (*d*) Psycholinguistics, (*e*) Experimental phonetics, (*f*) Romance, *or* Germanic, *or* Slavonic philology. 5. Advanced linguistic theory (including a study of the major contemporary schools). 6. The structure of English. 7. One of: (*a*) The structure of French, (*b*) The German language, (*c*) The Italian language, (*d*) The structure of another language (subject to approval). 8. A special subject taken in another department, e.g. Social Anthropology, Psychology of Communication and Thought. The third year of the course is spent abroad at a University Institution: students study the language chosen under 7 and a further language or dialect previously unknown to them. During this year, they write a short thesis on some aspect of the new language or dialect. In addition, all students are examined in their second year in Comparative Philology, practical phonetics, and practical linguistic analysis.
Linguistics in Combined Subject courses. Courses in French and Linguistics, German and Linguistics, and Italian and Linguistics

extend over ten terms, including a year abroad. In addition to the Linguistics courses, there are two papers of a linguistic nature associated with the history or synchronic description of the language concerned. The final examination for the Linguistics component consists of: 1. Phonetics and phonology. 2. Linguistic theory and the history of linguistics. 3. One of the options (a)–(e) described above. An approved thesis is written during the year abroad.

Courses in English Literature and Linguistics, Latin and Linguistics, Psychology and Linguistics, and Philosophy and Linguistics extend over seven terms (i.e. no year abroad). All involve the same two basic papers, in Phonetics and Phonology, and in Linguistic theory and the history of linguistics. The English Literature combination in addition involves one of the options (a)–(e), and a course in the structure of English. The Latin combination involves one of the options (a)–(e), and a course in Comparative philology (Romance and Indo-European). The Psychology combination involves a paper on Child language acquisition, and a project. The Philosophy combination involves a further two options from the following: (a) Sociolinguistics and dialectology, (b) The structure of English, (c) Child language acquisition, (d) Advanced linguistic theory.

2. *University of York* (details from the 1971–2 Prospectus, pp. 65–8, and from the brochure of the Language Department).

'Language' includes linguistics, the psychology and sociology of linguistic behaviour, the study of exotic and of European languages, and a variety of options taken either within the department or in another department, e.g. Biology, Computation, English and related European literatures, Mathematics, Philosophy, Physics, Sociology. The duration of Single Subject and Main courses, except for English Philology students, is normally four years. The second year is normally spent at a continental university, or (in the case of English language students) at an immigrant centre in Britain, on V.S.O. teaching abroad, or some similar work. Honours degrees are awarded for either Single Subject or Combined Subject degrees, all of equal academic standing. Single Subject students are examined in the following ten subjects; 1. Psychological and sociological aspects of linguistic behaviour. 2. General and descriptive linguistics. 3. Historical and comparative linguistics. 4 & 5. Competence in, and structure and history of, a language not previously studied. 6 & 7. Advanced competence in, and structure and history of a language already studied for G.C.E. 'A' level or similar examination, or in 'English and related Germanic languages'. 8, 9 & 10. Options within the department or in another department; if 'English and related Germanic languages' has not been offered for papers 6 and 7, paper 8 must be 'The structure of Modern English'. The language for papers 4 and 5 may be chosen from list A below, and that for papers 6 and 7 from list B:

A: Chinese, Hindi, Pali, Russian, Sanskrit, Sinhalese, Swahili.

B: Chinese, 'English and related Germanic languages', French, German, Spanish.

Students offering Language as a Main Subject are examined in subjects 1 to 7 and take a subsidiary subject in another department; those taking Language in equal combination take subjects 1 to 5 in Language and an equal load elsewhere; those offering Language as a subsidiary take subjects 1 to 3 and a main subject elsewhere. 'English and related Germanic languages' includes a study of Old, Middle and Modern English, Creole English, and one other Germanic language, e.g. Swedish. Language is offered as a Combined Subject degree with English, Education, Philosophy and Mathematics. Among the other options normally available are acoustic phonetics, psychology and learning theory, theories of meaning, the sociolinguistic study of a particular community, computation, pidgin and creole languages, the preparation of language teaching materials. Special arrangements are made where necessary for overseas students. The department has a particular commitment to the study of bilingualism and multilingualism and the political, cultural, economic and educational problems of multilingual communities. It also works in close collaboration with the Language Teaching Centre, which specializes in the application of modern linguistics and learning theory to language teaching and the training of modern language teachers.

3. *University of London* (details from the Calendars and departmental prospectuses, 1973–4).

The Department of Phonetics and Linguistics at the School of Oriental and African Studies, the Department of Linguistics at University College, and the Department of Language Study at the London School of Economics have collaborated in planning the course in Linguistics, and have arrangements whereby students from one department can attend lectures given in another, especially for the special subjects. The Linguistics part of the final examination consists of either four or five papers from the following, the first three being compulsory. 1. Principles of linguistics: descriptive, comparative and historical. 2. General linguistic theory I: grammar, semantics. 3. General linguistic theory II: phonetics, phonology. 4, 5. *One* or *two* of the following, depending on the degree course chosen: (a) Phonetics, (b) Historical linguistics, (c) Linguistic typology and language classification, (d) Linguistics and language teaching, (e) Linguistics and the study of literature, (f) Sociolinguistics: language and the community, (g) Psycholinguistics: language and the individual. All students take a practical test in phonetics.

At the School of Oriental and African Studies, two-subject B.A. Honours degrees are offered in an African language and Linguistics, and Social Anthropology and Linguistics, and other combinations are envisaged. General linguistics also forms part of the courses for the B.A. in an African language and anthropology, and the B.A. South East Asian Studies degrees in anthropology and in psychology. Examples of special undergraduate courses offered are: introduction to the phonetics of South East Asian, Turkic, or African languages; introduction to the descriptive analysis of a selected Asian, African, or American Indian language.

At the London School of Economics, the department provides teaching for a number of two-subject combinations for the degree of B.A., namely, Linguistics and one Modern Language (French, German, Russian), and two Modern Languages (French/Russian, French/Spanish, German/French, German/Russian, and German/Spanish). It is emphasised that, as the total number of places at the School for degrees in Language Studies is small, preference is given to applicants for the Linguistics courses. Students taking two languages are required to attend courses in General linguistics and Phonetics. The duration of courses is four years, the third year being spent abroad.

At University College, B.A. degrees are available in French and Linguistics, German and Linguistics, Philosophy and Linguistics, English and Linguistics, and Anthropology and Linguistics.

A three- or four-year course in Russian and Linguistics is offered at the School of Slavonic and East European Studies.

4. *University of Edinburgh* (details from the Calendar, 1973-4).

For the ordinary degree of M.A. (from 1971, called B.A.), one studies not less than five subjects, comprising three 'single' (i.e. one-year) courses, and two 'double' (i.e. two-year) courses. There is a first-year course, Linguistics I, and a second-year course, Lingusitics II, the first of which counts as a 'single' for the Ordinary degree, and both of which together constitute a double course for this degree. The course covers an introduction to phonetics, phonology, grammar, and semantics; there is also a brief treatment of the history of linguistics, comparative linguistics, and the role of language in society. The phonetics component consists of an introduction to general phonetics, including problems of phonetic notation, and a detailed study of the pronunciation of English. M.A. with Honours is available in the following Joint Degrees. French and Linguistics (Faculty of Arts) is a four-year course, the third year of which is spent in a French-speaking country; the final examination comprises nine papers, including a paper on linguistic theory, two half-papers chosen from a range of options (e.g. Applied linguistics, Sociolinguistics, Experimental phonetics), a half-paper on French linguistics, two papers on Romance linguistics, and a paper on linguistic theory in relation to French. German and Linguistics is also a four-year course, with the third year spent abroad in a German-speaking country; the final examination comprises ten subjects, including a paper on linguistic theory, two option half-papers (as with French), a long essay on a linguistics subject, and a paper on linguistic theory in relation to German. English Language and Linguistics is a four-year course, whose examination includes two papers on linguistic theory, and a paper on linguistic theory in relation to English. Russian and Linguistics includes a paper on linguistic theory, one on linguistic theory in relation to Russian, and two papers from a range of subjects including Comparative Slavonic philology, Modern Russian, historical phonetics and grammar of Russian, Polish, and Serbo-Croat. The course in Philosophy and Linguistics includes two papers on linguistic theory and one paper on linguistics and philosophy. Social Anthropology and Linguistics, and Psychology and Linguistics are four-year courses taught in the Faculty of Social Sciences. The former includes in its final examination two papers on linguistic theory, one on linguistics and anthropology, and a dissertation on an approved subject. The latter's examination involves six written papers, including one on linguistic theory, one on psycholinguistics, one on the psychology of language (advanced), and a thesis submitted on an individual research project in either Psychology or Linguistics.

5. *University College of North Wales, Bangor* (details from the 1973–4 Handbook, pp. 91–3).

Honours B.A. degrees are taken in two stages, a Part One, which normally occupies the whole of the first year, and a Part

Two, which occupies the remaining years of study. All students take three subjects for Part One, and Linguistics may be one of these. Three courses are taken: 1. Introduction to descriptive linguistics. 2. Introduction to phonetics. 3. Introduction to historical linguistics and language variety.

Candidates may then proceed to specialize in Linguistics, taking a B.A. Joint Honours degree in Linguistics and French, German, Russian, Italian (all of which involve a year abroad, i.e. a further three years of study after Part One), English, Welsh, Philosophy, and Psychology (a further two years of study after Part One). All students take five courses in Linguistics: 1. Phonetics and phonology. 2. Linguistic theory and grammatical analysis. 3. Semantics. 4. Two of: (*a*) Historical linguistics, (*b*) Language varieties, (*c*) Applied linguistics. 5. In the case of French, German, Russian and Italian, there is a course on the structure of English and one on the structure of the foreign language being studied; in the case of English, Philosophy and Psychology, there is a course on the structure of English; in the case of Welsh and Linguistics, one may take either a single course on the structure of Welsh, or two courses on the structure of Welsh and the structure of English.

Honours in Linguistics (single subject) involves: 1–3 above. 4. Historical linguistics. 5. Language varieties. 6. The structure of English. 7. The stucture of a second language. 8. Additional linguistic theory. 9. One of: (*a*) Applied linguistics, (*b*) The structure of a third language, (*c*) A special approved subject. 10. A dissertation. The Part Two course extends over three sessions, the second of these normally being spent abroad.

6. *University of Lancaster* (details taken from the Linguistics prospectus of the Department of English, 1972–3, with 1974 modifications incorporated).

Linguistics is offered as one of three subjects for Part I of the B.A. Honours Degree, taken in the first year. In Part II of the degree, Linguistics may be offered as a Combined Major degree with Classical Studies, English, French Studies, Russian Studies (available in 3- and 4-year courses), and Philosophy; also as a minor subject for degrees in Classics, English, French Studies, Russian and Soviet Studies, Philosophy, Sociology, Computer Studies. Further combinations (e.g. Linguistics and German) are planned, and Linguistics and Czechoslovak Studies, and Educational Studies and Linguistics are now available. The Part I course is a general introduction to the main areas of descriptive and theoretical linguistics, including phonetics. Students take four courses for their Part II, from a range including transformational grammar, sociolinguistics and field methods, semantics, general phonetics, linguistics in relation to a language other than English, and theoretical linguistics.

7. *University of Birmingham* (details from a Linguistics Department brochure, 1973).

Linguistics may be studied as part of a Combined Honours degree with French, German, Greek (Ancient or Modern), Italian, Latin, Russian, and Spanish. Ancient Greek and Latin are three-year courses; students of Russian who do not have this subject at A-level spend the first year on preliminary Russian in addition to a further three years; the remaining combinations are four-year courses. An ancillary language is studied in the first two years, probably from the following: French, German, Ancient Greek, Italian, Latin, Portuguese, Russian, Serbo-Croat, Spanish. The final examination includes papers on linguistic theory, the ancillary language, developments in linguistics, semantics and stylistics, philology (Classical, Germanic, Romance, or Slavonic), and a project.

8. *University of Leeds* (details from a brochure issued by the Department of Linguistics, 1973).

There is both a Linguistics and a Phonetics Department at

Leeds, and they combine to produce one-half of a number of three-year degree courses: Arabic, Chinese, French, and Spanish are currently available. Courses include an introduction to language and linguistics, linguistic theory, sociolinguistics, stylistics, comparative studies in linguistics, and phonetics. It is a main aim of the course to integrate the study of linguistic theory with the intensive study of a foreign language.

9. A number of other courses involving a main element of Linguistics are available. At the University of Essex, the Language Centre offers courses in Linguistics, French and English; and Linguistics, Russian and English. There is a Combined degree in Russian and Linguistics at the New University of Ulster. A B.Sc. course in Communication Science and Linguistics is offered at the University of Aston. And, following the recommendation of the Speech Therapy Report mentioned in the Preface that all future training of speech therapists should be at degree level, a number of degree courses in speech therapy are planned. A B.Ed. in Speech has in fact been available for some years at the University of Newcastle, and other courses (under various titles) are proposed or under way, e.g. at Aberdeen (Robert Gordons Institute of Technology), Birmingham (Polytechnic), Glasgow (Jordanhill College of Education), and Manchester. At Reading, a four-year B.A. course specifically on Linguistics and Language Pathology will begin in 1975.

10. *University of Surrey* (details taken from the Prospectus, 1974–5, pp. 85–6.)
There is a four-year degree course in Linguistics and Regional Studies, though 'Linguistics' here covers far more than the sense described in this book, as it includes the notion of proficiency in a foreign language. The practical aim of the course is 'to furnish industry, commerce, the professions, public and international organizations, etc. with graduates who are highly skilled in the use of a foreign language, have a thorough knowledge of the

region where that language is spoken, and have specialized in a special study of contemporary vocational significance and have been trained to apply this to their language area' (p. 85). Each course has three main components, Language and Linguistic Studies, Regional Studies, and Special Studies. One main language is studied (German and Russian at present, with French proposed in 1975), and an optional subsidiary language is available (French or Swedish). In the language programmes, emphasis is placed upon linguistic analysis, the study of specialist terminologies, translation study, stylistics, foreign-language seminars, oral practice and techniques. There is a course in General Linguistics in the first two years, in which students are introduced to the nature of language, its social and cultural context, its function and structure. This provides a foundation for descriptive and contrastive linguistics applied to the main and subsidiary languages. The aim of the Regional Studies component is 'a thorough acquaintance with the contemporary scene in the foreign-language area and a more specialized knowledge of its economics, law, politics, or problems of applied geography' (p. 85). The Special Studies component selects from Economics, Geography, International Relations, and Law. A final-year option in Linguistics is available, and project work while abroad may also involve linguistic topics.

Index